T0114192

Praise for *After You Die*

"I've known Frank Santora for many years, and I've always appreciated the way he presents truth so simply and authentically. Frank's book *After You Die* certainly reflects that quality as he tackles a complex subject in a way that's both logical and easy to understand. Why does it take more faith for people to believe that God *doesn't* exist than to believe that He does? Can we know what happens after we die? And is there more than one path to God? Frank thoroughly answers these all-important questions that affect each reader's eternal destiny. If you're not sure how to answer those questions for yourself or in your conversations with others, this book will serve as a valuable resource."

—Rick Renner, author and senior pastor
of the Moscow Good News Church

"In *After You Die,* Frank Santora takes on a complex and serious topic—a topic that is hard to talk about, yet everyone faces—and makes it thoroughly engaging and completely entertaining. It's filled with incredible scientific wonder about the human body, as well as awe-inspiring, life-changing spiritual truths. This book awakened my heart, mind, and soul to reach up and out . . . to look beyond just the finite things that my eyes can see . . . and to discover the hope and the beauty of the yet to be seen! Through the pages of this book you can see the glorious!"

—Alvin Slaughter, gospel recording artist
and founder of Alvin Slaughter International

"Pastor Frank Santora's book *After You Die* is a book for everyone, believer and nonbeliever. Pastor Frank masterfully and colorfully gets people's attention on what the afterlife is going to be like. If you have questions about life, what you can do to prepare, and what's in store, I highly recommend this book."

—Anthony Storino, senior pastor
of Abundant Grace Church

"I'm excited about Frank Santora's book *After You Die* and believe you will be too. It takes an honest, thought-provoking look at the subject we all must deal with, but none of us really want to face—our own mortality. But more than that, Frank answers the tough questions that inevitably surround this subject in a candid, straightforward, and no-nonsense way that I admire and appreciate. You will be challenged and inspired as you weigh the evidence for yourself. This is a must-read for the believer and unbeliever alike!"

—Jesse Duplantis, founder of Jesse Duplantis Ministries

"Perception transcends all aspects of human existence, including death. The way we view life's end will determine our anticipation of it. William Penn's insightful but simple saying that 'Death is no more than a turning of us over from time to eternity' corresponds with Frank Santora's work *After You Die*. Santora's candid, yet uncomplicated philosophy of death addresses the subject's commonly asked questions while providing a sense of hope in the hereafter. The uncomplicated but profound principles shared in this book will equip you when encouraging the bereaved or just when conversing on this age-old, controversial topic. I highly recommend this book—it is a must-read."

—Dr. Kingsley Fletcher, His Majesty Drolor Bosso Adamtey I of the Se (Shai) Traditional Area in Ghana, West Africa

After You Die

Unveiling the Mysteries of Heaven

FRANK SANTORA

New York Nashville London Toronto Sydney New Delhi

Howard Books
A Division of Simon & Schuster, Inc.
1230 Avenue of the Americas
New York, NY 10020

Copyright © 2012 by Frank Santora

All rights reserved, including the right to reproduce this book or portions thereof in any form whatsoever. For information address Howard Books Subsidiary Rights Department, 1230 Avenue of the Americas, New York, NY 10020.

First Howard Books paperback edition September 2012

HOWARD and colophon are trademarks of Simon & Schuster, Inc.

Scripture quotations marked (NIV) are taken from THE HOLY BIBLE, NEW INTERNATIONAL VERSION®, NIV®. Copyright © 1973, 1978, 1984 by Biblica US, Inc.® Used by permission.

Scripture quotations marked (NKJV) are taken from the New King James Version. Copyright © 1982 by Thomas Nelson, Inc. All rights reserved. Used by permission.

Scripture quotations marked (NLT) are taken from the Holy Bible, New Living Translation, copyright © 1996, 2004, 2007. Used by permission of Tyndale House Publishers Inc., Carol Stream, Illinois 60188. All rights reserved.

Scripture taken from The Message. Copyright © 1993, 1994, 1995, 1996, 2000, 2001, 2002. Used by permission of NavPress Publishing Group.

Scripture quotations marked (KJV) are taken from the King James Version of the Holy Bible. The KJV is in the public domain.

Scripture quoted by permission. All scripture quotations, unless otherwise indicated, are taken from the NET Bible® copyright ©1996–2006 by Biblical Studies Press, L.L.C. www.bible.org. All rights reserved. This material is available in its entirety as a free download or online Web use at http://www.netbible.org.

Scripture quotations marked (GNT) are taken from the Good News Translation of the Holy Bible, Good News Translation® (Today's English Version, Second Edition). Copyright © 1992 American Bible Society. All rights reserved.

For information about special discounts for bulk purchases, please contact Simon & Schuster Special Sales at 1-866-506-1949 or business@simonandschuster.com.

The Simon & Schuster Speakers Bureau can bring authors to your live event. For more information or to book an event, contact the Simon & Schuster Speakers Bureau at 1-866-248-3049 or visit our website at www.simonspeakers.com.

Designed by Kyoko Watanabe

Manufactured in the United States of America

10 9 8 7 6 5 4 3 2 1

Library of Congress Cataloging-in-Publication Data
Santora, Frank.
After you die : unveiling the mysteries of heaven / Frank Santora.
p. cm.
Includes bibliographical references.
1. Future life—Christianity. 2. Heaven—Christianity. 3. Death—Religious aspects—Christianity. I. Title.
BT903.S26 2012
236'.2—dc23 2011050294

ISBN 978-1-4165-9731-5
ISBN 978-1-4391-8277-2 (ebook)

In loving memory of my grandfather and grandmother, John and Jennie Sommese, who I know are smiling down from heaven in love upon me. I miss you both but will see you again someday.

Contents

PART IV:
Hell, No! (You Don't Want to Go)

PART V:
Heaven

PART VI:
Me: How Should Eternity Affect My Now?

PART VII:

Jesus: Is He the Only Way?

PART VIII:

Hope

PART I

The Truth We All Must Face

CHAPTER 1

Grandpa and JFK Jr.

My grandfather was a man's man. I remember him being big and strong, even with the prosthetic leg he had from the knee down. When he put it on, he would say, "It's time for me to become the Bionic Man," and back then I believed he really had a super-robot leg like Steve Austin on the TV show.

He adored his grandkids. There were five of us: myself, my sister and brother, and my two cousins who lived next door. Whenever my grandfather came over, he would show up with gifts for all of us. And not just little gifts—he went all out. One day he showed up with Kick 'N Go scooters, the kind with a pedal on the back that you'd stomp to propel the scooter. These were the toys of all toys back in the day and cost about a hundred dollars each. My grandfather bought five of them: one for each kid. I'm sure the neighbors thought he was spoiling us, but he didn't care. He loved us, and we loved him.

Sometimes I would go and spend the night with Grandpa and Grandma at their home in Brooklyn. On those nights when he came home from work, he'd bring this huge hero sandwich from a deli, the largest sandwich you ever saw, and he'd hold it up in front of the two of us. Then he'd start eating from one end and I'd start eating from the other, and we'd have a race to the middle of that hero sandwich.

As you can imagine, he was my hero. He was Grandpa, and there was nobody more alive than he was.

One morning my parents came into my room and woke me

up. But they were not as happy and jovial as usual. They sat down on my bed and told me something I didn't want to believe, that I couldn't believe. Grandpa had died.

Grandpa? Big, strong, happy Grandpa? He was gone? It didn't happen, it couldn't happen, not to Grandpa.

I was eleven years old and my grandfather was dead. It was the first loss of my life, and a pain hit me that I had never felt before.

But he was only the first.

Over the years I experienced other deaths. My cousin John, who was like a brother to me, died of cancer not two years later. My grandmother, Grandpa's wife for thirty-eight years and widow for nineteen more.

I know this is sad, but hang on. There's a point.

I've seen other deaths, too. As a pastor, I get called to preach at funerals. I get called to go to hospital rooms and emergency rooms and talk to people who are dying and to the people they leave behind.

Death is a part of my life.

Guess what? It's part of yours, too.

Who's Got a Ticket?

Remember those ticket machines you see at bakeries and ice-cream shops? The sign says TAKE A NUMBER, and when you come in, you grab that little ticket and stand around, trying to find something to do, until the clerk calls out your number. You hand the guy your ticket, give him your order, and then all in a rush you're done and out of there.

Well, the moment you were born, you grabbed a ticket. And no matter how you spend your time kicking around in this world, finding something to do, at some point you're gonna have to give up that ticket. You're done, and you're out of here.

Bam.

Just like that.

A few years ago I turned on the TV and saw pictures of a small private plane next to images of John F. Kennedy Jr. "Plane missing, presumed dead," the caption read. Pretty soon the presumed became fact. The heir to the Kennedy legacy, a handsome young man whose life and political and business future were constantly mused about by media stars and pundits, was dead. Gone. Life over, story over, musing over. All that fame, fortune, and favored-son glory didn't mean a thing when his plane slammed into the ocean.

You see, it doesn't matter if you're a hero to your grandson. It doesn't matter if you're a boy who beat cancer as a baby, a grandmother who cooked unbelievable lasagna, or even the famous golden boy of the political world. You are going to die. And you don't know when.

As they say in the movies, "Nobody gets out of here alive."

CHAPTER 2

Don't Be a Fool

JESUS TOLD A story about the certainty of death, and if he told it today, it would sound something like this:

Once upon a time, there was a businessman, a real wheeler-dealer. Everything he set his mind to do he succeeded at doing. If he bought a stock, he paid pennies and within a week sold for dollars. If he put up a high-rise, there'd be a boom in new businesses needing office space. If he dug an oil well, there'd be a revolution in the Middle East and oil would go through the roof. He was so successful that Donald Trump wanted to be *his* apprentice.

Well, this guy was working hard, doing his thing and amassing so much wealth that he was paying Bill Gates to do his taxes, when he suddenly came to an epiphany. "Hey," he said, "I am the richest guy in the world. I can buy anything I want, do anything I want, hire anybody I want. Nothing and no one can stop me. What the heck—I'm gonna live it up from here on out. The whole world is mine for the buying; in fact, that's just what I'm going to do, starting first thing tomorrow morning. I'm going to secure all my investments, make sure I'm set forever, and then, look out, world—you're *mine*." And he went to bed laughing and dreaming about the life he was going to enjoy.

And that night . . . he died.

The end.

Great story, isn't it?

What? You don't think it's a great story?

Come on! Add in a gorgeous wife, two kids, a dog, and weekends at the country club, and you've got the American dream. Hey, even I like it.

Well, except for the death part. Nobody likes that.

You see, not only is this story the American dream, in Jesus' day it was the Israelite dream. All the Israelite heroes were rich guys. Just look at the list:

Abraham—real-estate tycoon who snapped up the whole of Canaan
Jacob—savvy livestock mogul
Joseph—prime minister, economic prognosticator, and financial genius
David—poor boy who made good, became the leader of the nation *and* a Top 40 rock star
Solomon—Richest king ever.

The Israelites *loved* a rich guy. They all wanted to *be* the rich guy.

So Jesus tells this story about a guy who does everything he's supposed to do in life when it comes to achieving success—everything the Israelites believed *they* were supposed to do. They're thinking, *Yep, that's what I want. Success. Riches. Everything.* And then the guy dies.

You can bet Jesus' listeners didn't care for the story, either.

Oh, Jesus added an important bit. There was one other actor involved: God.

According to Jesus, the story ends this way: And God looked down and said, "You fool. Tonight your soul is required of you" (see Luke 12:16–20).

Ouch. When God says you are a fool, you are a fool.

Now I know some people are thinking that Jesus told this story to lecture everybody about being rich. They think Jesus was some kind of ancient anticorporate, antiglobalization, tax-the-rich agitator. *Yeah! A rich guy bites the dust! Right on, Jesus!*

Wrong. That wasn't Jesus' point at all.

You see, the guy in Jesus' story *didn't actually do anything wrong.* And Jesus doesn't say he did. Jesus doesn't say the guy lied or cheated or stole or mistreated his employees or even overpriced his goods. He just said the guy made money and took steps to protect it. Jesus doesn't even accuse the guy of neglecting charity, except maybe by implication. As far as Jesus' listeners were concerned, the story was about an honest businessman climbing the ladder of success right to the top, just like Abraham, Jacob, Joseph, and all their other heroes. And then God calls the man a fool, and the man dies.

So, as they say, "What's up with *that*?"

At this point the anti-rich people pop in. They say that because the guy was selfish and kept all his money, God called him a fool and killed him on the spot.

Wrong again.

God didn't say, "*Because* you are a fool, your soul is required of you." God didn't say, "*Because* you are rich, your soul is required of you." God didn't say, "*Because* you are proud and selfish, your soul is required of you." It wasn't *punishment.* It was just a statement of fact. The man's number was up. His ticket was called. His bucket was kicked. There was no *because* whatsoever. It was just his *time.* If the man had been a pauper or a preacher or a teacher or a hermit in Timbuktu, it wouldn't have mattered. His life was over because life on earth ends. *Bam.* Just like that.

So why did God call the man a fool?

Jesus gave the answer as a very blunt question—"What profit is it to a man if he gains the whole world, and loses his own soul?" (Matt. 16:26 NKJV).

Jesus wasn't saying that because the man was wealthy he had lost his soul. Jesus was saying he was a fool because he neglected to deal with the reality of his own mortality. The man was a fool because he ignored death.

You see, the wealth, the big house, the hot spouse, the great kids, the faithful dog, and the country club may all be great things, but when death comes the entire universe says, "So what?" as it kicks you out the door.

Hearses don't come with trailer hitches.

There's a verse in the Bible that would probably rank as everyone's least favorite, and it goes like this: "It is appointed unto men once to die" (Heb. 9:27 KJV). I don't know about you, but I'd rather skip that particular appointment. Do you think we could call God and reschedule? But no, other translations don't even allow us the fiction of that idea. They put it even more bluntly: "Everyone must die" (Heb. 9:27 GNT).

Ouch. No wiggle room there. Don't you wish it said "Everyone but you must die?" Or maybe "Everyone we don't know and love must die."

But it doesn't say that. It says, "Everyone must die."

This is the truth we all must face: one hundred out of one hundred people who ever live die. Yes, including rich people. Including cute little babies. Including lovable old people. Including handsome, dynamic pastors. (I'm none too happy about that one. You'd think we'd get an exception.)

And whether we like it or not, the Bible is telling us we *must* deal with that fact.

In his story, Jesus was saying, "Listen up! I don't care how good you are at everything else in life. I don't care if you're roaring up the corporate ladder like King Kong on a skyscraper. If you don't deal with death, you are an utter fool."

You see, it is foolish not to consider death and all its implications. It's like driving down the road in the dark with the headlights off and your eyes closed, hoping that if you have the radio turned up loud enough, nothing bad will happen.

CHAPTER 3

Religion, Politics, and Death

I'M SURE YOU know the story of the steamship *Titanic*. Everybody knows how it struck the iceberg and sank, killing over 1,500 people in the worst ocean disaster in recorded history.

But did you know the disaster needn't have happened at all?

The *Titanic* received several warnings that icebergs were in the area. The captain made a course change at the first warning, and then, convinced all was safe, went to dinner. Later warnings that the *Titanic* had actually steered *toward* the iceberg were completely ignored by the crew—the captain wasn't even informed.[1]

But even steaming on without precautions, the *Titanic* still had a chance to survive. You see, the ship was *designed* to handle a head-on collision. The inside of the hull was divided into sixteen airtight compartments, so that if up to four were punctured and filled with water, the air in the rest of the compartments would keep the ship afloat. Edward Wilding, an expert on the ship's design, testified in the accident investigation that a head-on impact would certainly have killed crewmen in the forward areas, but the ship would have stayed afloat and even made it to harbor.[2]

But the *Titanic* didn't meet the iceberg head-on. At the last minute, with the iceberg dead ahead, the bridge officer did what most of us do when death finally looms in front of us, big and ugly and undeniable: he tried to avoid it. He ordered the ship to turn away from the iceberg. But it was too late. The iceberg was too close. And instead of hitting the iceberg head-on, the *Titanic* raked alongside the iceberg like a car sideswiping a semi. The iceberg cut through nearly the entire hull from bow to midship, flooding water into six of the interior compartments, sealing the ship's fate.[3] All because the crew ignored the warning signs and tried to avoid the inevitable.

It is foolish to ignore the warnings about death.

It is foolish to try to avoid it.

Oh, but it's so easy to avoid things, isn't it?

My father-in-law was always a thin, athletic, picture-of-health type guy. He never went to the doctor because he never needed to. But not long ago he started gaining weight. Perhaps that's not unusual for older men, but his weight gain was a little odd. Everything was centered in his stomach, nowhere else, and it kept getting larger. He looked as if he had swallowed a basketball. My mother-in-law kept telling him that his weight gain didn't look normal, that he needed to see a doctor, but he refused. He didn't need a doctor, he claimed—he was okay, it would turn out fine. This went on for months, until at last he consented and went to the hospital. There we found out he had a huge internal cyst, and the tests showed it was cancerous. He needed immediate surgery to remove the cancer.

Fortunately, the surgery was successful. But what did the doctors tell my father-in-law before they started? "This should have been dealt with sooner."

How many times can we say that in life? "This should have been dealt with sooner" could be a statement made about almost all the problems we face.

You may recall the very recent NFL lockout as team owners and players fought over everything from salary caps to free-agent contracts—problems that everyone knew were there but nobody wanted to deal with.

Or the 2008 mortgage crisis that had actually been building since the late 1970s—problems that everyone knew were there but nobody wanted to deal with.

Or, perhaps closer to home, how about the growing silence and neglect in a marriage that blows up into a horrible divorce because of problems that everyone knew about but nobody wanted to deal with?

Begin to sound familiar?

The Unavoidable Topic

The unavoidable truth is that the longer you wait to deal with a problem like death, the more likely you will be unable to deal with it when it finally comes.

And remember, it finally comes. And when it does, it's final.

For everyone.

So why do people avoid dealing with death?

They Don't Want to Deal with the Added Pressure

Life is full of pressure, isn't it? "I've got bills to pay, taxes, a mortgage, children who need food and clothes and cell phones. My wife says I work too much, my boss says I don't work hard enough, and my mother-in-law says both. And now you're saying I have to worry about death, too? Well, death can back off!"

Trouble is, death doesn't back off. Instead, it steps closer with every tick of the clock. Remember the Terminator, the evil killer robot played by Arnold Schwarzenegger? No matter what the heroes tried to do to stop it, it just kept coming. It was relentless. Even if it seemed stymied for a moment, it just said, "I'll be back." That's death. The ultimate pressure.

They Don't Want to Deal with What It Means for Their Lives

Death has a way of calling you out. Like the villain in almost every action movie you'll ever see, death demands that the hero "show his stuff." And if any of that "stuff" isn't up to the challenge, death kicks it out of the way. For us, all that "stuff" is the wasted time and energy in our lives that in the end don't matter. But we don't want to admit that anything like that is going on. We *like* our stuff. We don't want to look at it in light of death. That might mean we have to change—and nobody wants to do that.

They Don't Know What Comes Next

That's the real biggie, isn't it? If we don't face death, we can believe all sorts of things about life and what comes after. We can believe we're never going to die. (Don't laugh. Most people seem to go through life just that way. Jesus' rich fool did.) We can believe, *Oh, it'll all work out.* We can believe, *It just ends. Pfft. Like falling asleep.* We can believe, *Well, I'm a good person, so I'm going to be in heaven.* We can even believe, *All my fun friends will be in hell, so I'm going there.* But the truth is that none of those beliefs come from knowing anything at all about death. Those are the answers of flippant avoidance. They are, as God says, the words of a fool.

No, to truly face death we have to deal with all these things soberly and thoughtfully. There is a question we must answer: What *does* happen thirty seconds after you die?

Or, to put it another way: Do we keep on living? Is there life after death?

Do we have a *soul*?

PART II

The Soul: Does It Exist?

CHAPTER 4

Grandma Wasn't There

I REMEMBER THE DAY of my grandmother's funeral. All my family and I gathered on a Brooklyn city street outside the funeral home. We were there in anticipation of going in to see the body of our grandmother, whom we had all loved so dearly. The last time I had seen her was when she was still alive. She had been full of faith and encouragement, believing in God and believing that the best was going to happen. She was still vibrant even though she was in a hospital bed. Her face had had its full color—she was Grandma. That was the picture in my mind's eye. When I walked into the funeral home, that's what I expected to see.

When the family went in to see my grandmother, I was with my cousin. I remember my uncle, her son, kneeling by the open casket, rubbing her hand the whole time. But when I looked in the coffin, I didn't see Grandma. I saw something that looked like Grandma, but it wasn't her. She wasn't there.

THE BREATH OF LIFE

As I said before, one of my duties is to preside over funerals for the people of my congregation. That involves speaking, yes, but it also means I am there to comfort family members as they grieve over their loved ones. So I've gone into a lot of funeral homes and looked at a lot of bodies. The one thing I can tell you is that no matter who they are, when I look at their bodies, I know they're not there. They don't even look there. The body is still there, but the person is gone.

What does that tell us?

It tells us that there was a part of the person that was giving the body life, and it had to leave the body.

Very early in the Bible, God says that the body and life are two very different things. "And the Lord God formed man of the dust of the ground"—that is, God formed man's body—"and then breathed into his nostrils the breath of life; and man became a living being" (Gen. 2:7 NKJV). So the Bible seems to be saying that the body is not life at all. The body on its own is just dust in a fancy shape. It is a shell into which God must put something called "the breath of life" in order for it to live. Today we call that breath of life "the soul."

More Than a Machine

There are people who suggest that there is no soul. That the body is just a machine—that the body itself is life, and that's all there is to it. But if all we are is a body, how come we can see a body that has no life in it? If the body itself is life, then shouldn't it just "work"?

Like most of you, I have a car. I put fuel in the tank, I turn the key, the car starts, and it runs. Now suppose I run out of fuel in the tank. The car stops running, right? But is it "dead"? No, because all I have to do is put fuel back in, turn the key, and *vroom*! The car starts up again.

But with people, that doesn't work, does it? When a man's body stops running, we can't just shove a ham sandwich down his throat, twist his earlobe, and expect him to get up and start walking and talking again, can we? I like the movie *Frankenstein* as much as anyone, but you don't jump-start a body, lightning or no lightning. Nobody backs a Chevy up to Grandpa, plugs in the jumper cables, and gets him going again.

Ah, but the human body is more complicated than an automobile, you say. Okay, then, how about a nuclear-powered submarine? That's a complicated device, isn't it? Or a space shuttle? They don't call it rocket science for nothing. But all of these devices are dead things that can be more or less restarted at any moment with comparatively little effort. Even if you're not a rocket scientist, you probably understand that somewhere there is a list of steps for getting a rocket to fly. If anyone took those steps, they could bring even something as complex as a space shuttle "to life."

But that list apparently doesn't exist for human beings. Once our bodies stop working, that's the end of it. We're on or we're off, and if we're off, chances are we won't be on again.

The thing is, we know what keeps our bodies working when we're alive. We know we need food, water, and oxygen, and generally if we keep all three of those things going into our bodies at appropriate intervals our bodies will keep working. But when we die, simply putting those three things back into a body won't get it to start again. In fact, of those three only one is unquestionably used by doctors trying to revive a dying patient, and that is oxygen. I'm not a doctor, but I'm pretty confident that in a Code Blue situation, no physician yells, "Get him a hero sandwich, hold the mayo, stat!"

Recently, there was a news story about a woman who went into a coma after surgery. The doctors pronounced her brain-dead. Her body was working because they had her on a respirator, but her brain was gone. Shut down. Dead. Flatlining. The physicians told her husband that it was over, there was nothing they could do, and no point in keeping her body functioning without her mind. "Your wife is no longer here," they told him. She had been on the respirator for three days; it was time, they said, to turn it off. The husband asked that they shut down the machinery that kept her body working to allow the body to die on its own. They did as he requested.

And then, on her own, she woke up.

The doctors were amazed. They had no explanation for it. She was dead; her brain had no activity whatsoever. Their monitors were showing complete blanks. And nobody had done anything to revive her. Nobody gave her medicine. Nobody shocked her. Nobody pumped oxygen into her. Nobody poured water in her mouth or gave her so much as a bowl of chicken soup. In fact, they had just turned off all the equipment that had been "maintaining" her body. Yet without anyone turning so much as a virtual ignition key, she started to live again.[1]

So what happened? How could she be gone and just come back? What left? What came back?

Medical science has no explanation for it.

But the interesting thing is, humanity does. We always have. We call it *the soul.*

CHAPTER 5

Outside Evidence

NOW I KNOW the skeptic says that we just made up the concept of the soul. That's a Christian idea, to sell a certain form of religion and to make people feel better about death.

Except it isn't only a Christian idea. In fact, nearly all cultures throughout history have assumed that men and women have some sort of "life force," "spirit," or "soul"—some internal essence that is the answer to *why* a body that is living is so completely different and alien from one that is dead. The ancient pagans believed in a soul. The Greeks, Romans, Egyptians, Persians, and any other -ian or -ite you can think of all believed in a soul. And it's not just an ancient belief. Today the Jewish faith believes in a soul. Buddhists believe in a soul. Muslims, Japanese Shintoists, and Taoists believe in a soul. The Chinese believe in a soul and even go so far as to revere the souls of ancestors as minor gods. Even the most primitive "spirit" religions in the remote parts of the earth inherently assume the existence of a soul.

The only cultures that have rejected this notion are almost exclusively very modern ones based on the philosophy of atheism, usually in support of a dictatorship or totalitarian government system, that wish to avoid any conflict with the wishes of "the state." Even the individual atheist is most likely opposed to the concept based solely on rejecting the possibility of anything "supernatural" at all, because to accept that would be to accept the possibility of a supernatural God. If you don't want the latter, you can't risk accepting the former. But the evidence of humanity is clearly in favor of the soul.

The Evidence of Physics: Deeper Dimensions

I know that you may not be convinced by the evidence of continual human belief in the soul. I could quote the Bible, but maybe you doubt that the Bible is an authority on this issue. You say, "I can't see this thing you call a soul. I can't see any physical evidence for a soul. So what else is there?"

Well, how about the science of subatomic physics? Individual atoms cannot be seen, much less the particles that make them. Yet we firmly believe that these things exist.

"But we have evidence for them!" you say.

Yes. And we have evidence for the soul as well.

First, let's consider some of what physics currently teaches about the universe—the concept of dimensions.

Seeing in More Than Three Dimensions

I like going to movies. Lately, I've taken my son to a few action movies. These days they're all being made in 3-D. You walk into the theater and they hand you these plastic glasses. You put them on and they make the picture 3-D. What does *3-D* mean? It means the picture appears to have three dimensions: height and width but also depth, just like the book you are reading. We live in a three-dimensional world.

We also experience a fourth dimension—time. Things have an existence in time. There was a time when the book in your hands did not exist. Now it does. It is also getting older. There will eventually be a time when it no longer exists, when it crumbles into dust, not unlike us. We can see three of these dimensions in some way, and experience teaches us that the fourth is also there.

But physicists now theorize that there are other dimensions—up to *eleven* dimensions in total—that we can't see or experience.[1] No one can put on a special set of glasses and have them pop out before the eyes. No one can even detect them. In fact, aside from very complicated math problems, there really isn't any evidence to prove these dimensions exist. But many scientists believe they do.

I'm not going to argue whether they are correct or not—on that subject they are smarter than I am. But if we can accept the existence of things no one can see, feel, or detect, that are external to our experience of the world, why should the soul's existence be treated any differently? It shouldn't.

The Evidence of Testimony: Out-of-Body Experiences and NDEs

Well, what about science? If we admit the possibility of a soul, is there any scientific evidence for its existence?

Most atheists and even many believers would say, "No, there isn't."

They are both wrong.

You've probably heard about claims of those who have died temporarily and come back to life. Maybe you even know someone who has shared an experience with you—stories of a white light, a tunnel, seeing dead loved ones, and so on. Basically, somebody dies, usually in a hospital, and has an apparently supernatural experience before being revived by the hospital staff. Maybe you believe these are real, maybe not. Either way, you might be surprised to learn that medical science actually supports that these events can and do occur. They are officially called NDEs, or "near death experiences." Here are a few, collected by researchers and journalists—you may even recognize a few names among the subjects:

I died then. I felt my soul or something coming right out of my body, like you'd pull a silk handkerchief out of a pocket by one corner. It flew around and then came back and went in again and I wasn't dead anymore.

—*Ernest Hemingway, writer, describing what happened when he was caught in a bomb blast during World War I*[2]

Suddenly the pain, fever and acute distress seemed to evaporate. I was floating above my body, surrounded by soft blue light. I began to glide down a long tunnel, away from the bed . . . but suddenly I found myself back in my body. The doctors told me later that I had actually died for a time.

—*Donald Sutherland, actor, recalling a brush with death while being treated for meningitis in 1979*[3]

One day, during the course of play, [my grandson] said, "Grandma, when I died, I saw a lady." He was not yet three years old. I asked my daughter if anyone had mentioned anything to [him] about him dying, and she said, "No, absolutely not." But over the course of the next few months, he continued to talk about his experience. It was all during the course of play and in a child's vocabulary.

He said, "When I was in the doctor's car [the ambulance], the belt came undone, and I was looking down from above. . . . A lady came to take me . . . there were also many others who were getting new clothes, but not me, because I wasn't really dead. I was going to come back. . . . When you die, you see a bright lamp and . . . are connected by a cord."

—*A young child's NDE, related by his grandmother*[4]

There are literally thousands of such stories known, and millions more claimed. I think the child's account is particularly interesting. Not only had he not been told he had died, he had no awareness of what an NDE was or any notions on which to base his account.

Often the subject of an NDE will report that he was outside his physical body, usually floating above it, near the ceiling or in a corner. During this experience, he is conscious of who he is. He knows that he is looking at his own body and is aware that the body is dying, though he experiences no pain or discomfort. Many accounts describe people's seeing the doctors and nurses working and report specific words and unique actions. (One woman reported seeing a doctor accidentally kick a bucket and knock over a medical stand, though at the time she was in full cardiac arrest.)[5]

From this point, some report moving away from the body, even floating through the ceiling and outside, where eventually they begin traveling through a tunnel to a region of brilliant light and colors where they meet other people and encounter a powerful, loving Being. There may be a moment of "life review," where a person's good and bad actions in life are revealed. The person then arrives at a barrier or gate, through which he is denied passage and "sent back" to life. Note that the whole time the person is aware of who he is and often encounters family members or friends who have already died, recognizing them instantly.[6]

Fact or Fiction?

If you've heard of NDEs before, you may have heard the counterarguments: NDEs are "made up." "People see what they've been taught to see." "They're just a pop-culture fad." "NDEs are caused by oxygen deprivation or drug reactions."

The truth is, the counterarguments don't hold up.

Claim: NDEs Are Made Up

Truth: In 1982 a survey taken in the United States indicated that more than eight million people reported having had an NDE.[7] That's a lot of people to all be "making it up."

Claim: NDEs Are Just the Result of Religious and Cultural Beliefs

Truth: Studies have shown that regardless of culture, race, gender, faith, philosophy, or even age, people describe essentially the same core NDE elements in roughly the same way. Even people who do not profess a religion, including atheists, have reported NDEs.[8] Therefore, NDEs can't be a case of religious upbringing, nor does any major religion offer specific visual descriptions of the moments immediately following death.

Claim: NDEs Are Just a Modern Fad

Truth: The earliest NDE account comes from Plato. A famous painting by medieval artist Heironymus Bosch mimics NDE descriptions of a tunnel of light. Other NDE descriptions come to us from the sixteenth, eighteenth, and nineteenth centuries.[9]

Claim: NDEs Are Just the Effects of Oxygen Loss and Medical Side Effects

Truth: The effects of oxygen loss, resuscitative drugs, or ineffective anesthesia involve confusion, memory loss, and frightening, random imagery. NDE descriptions are completely the opposite and include intellectual clarity, good memory retention, pleasant images, a logical progression of events, and strong feelings of love and well-being.[10]

Furthermore, not all NDEs are associated with situations involving any of the suggested medical causes. NDEs have been triggered by situations of imminent danger, such as car crashes, mountain-climbing accidents, and the like. Others have occurred during deep meditation.[11]

Are NDEs Real?

Even if some specific activity in the brain can be attached to the NDE, Dr. Sam Parnia of Cornell University points out, this does not mean the experiences are "not real." After all, is love "real"? When I look at my daughter and my son, I feel great love for them. If you slap some electrodes to my head, you will see that my feelings coincide with a pattern of activity in my brain. Does that mean I don't actually love my children—that my love isn't "real"? Of course not. As Dr. Parnia notes, it is impossible to say whether the patterns cause the love or the love causes the patterns. But he also points out that if everything we do, see, think, or feel is merely the result of chemical patterns making us do, see, think, and feel these things, doesn't that mean we are just automatons?[12]

If that is the case, if I forget my wife's birthday or say, "Well, yes, that dress does make you look heavy," I can't be blamed for it. It's just the chemical patterns of my brain making me do and say those things. That's not going to wash with my wife, and I don't think it probably goes over with you, either. We have free will to do, say, and act as we choose. So whatever it is that makes me a "me," whatever it is that chooses to do the things I choose to do, is more than just random chemical patterns inside my head. Just as I am not merely my body, I am not merely my brain.

I am a soul.

CHAPTER 6

Inside Evidence

THE BIBLE SUPPORTS the view that we are neither simply our bodies nor simply our brains. In fact, the Bible doesn't just divide us into body and soul, it divides us into three parts. Those parts are the body, the spirit, and the soul.

In his very first letter, Paul makes an interesting statement that shows this evidence is biblical: "May your whole spirit, soul and body be kept blameless at the coming of our Lord Jesus Christ" (1 Thess. 5:23 NIV). Notice how Paul treats his readers as three-part beings. Just as the Bible teaches that God is a three-part being—the Trinity of the Father, the Son, and the Holy Spirit—it teaches that we, who are made "in his image," are also beings of three parts.

I like the way that Kenneth Hagin puts it: "Man is a spirit that possesses a soul that lives in a body."[1] Think about that idea. You are a spirit, and it is you. You have a soul, and it is you. And those two "yous" live in a body, and it also is you.

Let's take a moment to look at who those "yous" are.

DIVIDING SPIRIT AND SOUL

Up to now in this chapter we have only discussed the soul, but the spirit is also important, and just as distinct from the body. However, very few people today ever think of the spirit as something different from the soul. It's easy to think of the soul as separate from the body, especially from the "nebulous blob" point of view that Hollywood special-effects people make for films. There's the body, there's the soul (the blob), but what about the spirit? We don't have a handy Hollywood image for that one, so we dump it or lump it together with the soul.

So what are these elements? Why are they divided, and what is the purpose for each?

The Spirit of Man

The spirit is the dimension of man that deals with the spiritual realm. This is the part of man that contacts God and is eternal. When we use the word *soul* in modern-day speech, we typically are actually referring to the spirit. The Bible sometimes swaps the terms, or combines them into one term: "the inner man."

The Soul of Man

The soul of man is the dimension of man that deals with the mental realm. This is man's intellect—our sensibilities and our will. This is the part of man that reasons and thinks. Today we might say "mind" or "consciousness," though we often think of the soul and spirit together as one entity.

The Body of Man

The body of man is the one we know best. It is the dimension that deals with the physical realm. It is what allows our spirit and soul to exist in the world we know.

When I gave a sermon about this point, I decided to turn myself into a visual illustration of the concept. I had my staff order an astronaut costume, and we planned the service around a surprise appearance of me in this costume, complete with helmet and space suit, to start my sermon. Unfortunately, it never occurred to me to try the costume on before our Sunday morning services began. After all, it was a "One Size Fits All" costume—it said so on the label.

Five minutes before the sermon, I pulled the suit on only to discover it was "One Size Fits Most" and made of white spandex. It fit only in the sense that I could get my body into it and force the zipper closed. But it was too late to turn back. There was nothing I could do but slap on the helmet and walk out in front of the congregation in my space suit.

Did I mention it was white spandex?

Let's just say my church got to see a whole lot more of their pastor than anybody wanted to see. As for me, I really wanted to keep the helmet on and leave them thinking that somebody else on our staff was crazy enough to do this, and that I was just home sick in bed.

But I stuck with it. And the truth is, I think they got the point.

Maybe you do, too. Picture an astronaut in a space suit (hopefully not nearly as tight and embarrassing as mine). When you see that space suit floating outside the International Space Station, you may think, *That's an astronaut.* But are you really seeing the astronaut? No, all you're seeing is his space suit. The real man is inside the space suit. The suit exists merely to keep the real astronaut alive in a dangerous environment.

That's what our bodies are—they are our "earth suits." Their purpose is to keep the real "us" alive in a dangerous environment.

The Inner Man

Now even the Bible ties the soul and the spirit together; they may be separate parts, but they are still one being. And that corresponds with our modern tendency to lump them together. As I mentioned, the Bible calls the two elements of spirit and soul "the inner man" or "the innermost being." In other places, the Bible uses the term for soul—the Greek word *psyche*—as a catchall for both, such as in Acts 2: "And that day three thousand souls were added to them" (v. 41 NKJV). Well, that's not talking about three thousand minds, wills, and emotions; that's talking about three thousand spiritual beings who were added to the church. So depending on the use in Scripture, sometimes the soul is referring to the whole man, sometimes it's referring to the mind. It's usually fairly clear in context which it means, but the important thing to understand is that the two are also one, and what happens to one affects the other. And that applies to the body as well; hence the significance of Paul's prayer that all three remain strong and whole.

For the rest of this book, we will refer to the combined "innermost being" as *the soul.* Just remember that the term means both our spiritual nature and our intellectual selves.

CHAPTER 7

Hey, That Looks a Lot Like Me

So now we know that we die. And we know that when we die, a part of us that is not part of our bodies continues on, conscious and able to perceive its environment.

So what does it look like?

I think we need to keep in mind that saying what the soul looks like outside of the world we experience is a bit like trying to define color to a blind man. And we've also been affected by Hollywood, which as you recall loves to depict souls as nebulous blobs of colored light. I don't know about you, but I don't want to be a blob. I want to be *me*: hands, feet, head, fingers, toes; the whole package. By the way, I think that innate desire to go on being human is something to consider as a guide, too. And in reality, there is no cultural or scriptural basis for the idea that the soul is a nebulous blob of pretty lights.

So what does it look like? There are a few things we can glean from both the NDEs of others and the Word of God.

The Characteristics of the Soul

The Soul Is Immediately Recognizable

NDE accounts immediately acknowledge that the people know who they are. They also recognize the people they see during the experience as *people*. Look at the following account:

> About two weeks after the surgery, [my son] started asking when he could go back to the beautiful sunny place with all the flowers and animals. I said, "We'll go to the park in a few days, when you're feeling better." "No," he said, "I don't mean the park, I mean the sunny place I went to with the lady." I asked him, "What lady?" and he said, "The lady that floats. . . . You didn't take me there. The lady came and got me. She held my hand and we floated up. . . . You were outside when I was having my heart mended. . . . It was okay. The lady looked after me; the lady loves me. It wasn't scary; it was lovely. Everything was bright and colorful, [but] I wanted to come back to see you." [When he came back] "I was awake, but I was up on the ceiling, and when I looked down I was lying in a bed with my arms by my sides, and doctors were doing something to my chest. Everything was really bright, and I floated back down. . . ."
>
> One day I showed him a photo of my mum (she had passed away) when she was my age now, and he said, "That's her. That's the lady."
>
> —*The mother of a three-and-a-half-year-old who'd had open-heart surgery*[1]

Now notice that this testimony came from a very young child. Young children have no concept of the soul, and no preconceived notions of what a soul "should" look like. Most don't even understand the concept of death, and have no reason at all to think of dead people as looking like anything. If they've heard stories about "ghosts," they think of them as the sheet-over-the-head costumes from Halloween. Very young children also describe things in matter-of-fact, specific ways. If they see a ball, they call it a ball. If they see a pretty light, they call it a pretty light. If they see a person, they call him or her a person. They would not say a pretty light is a person even if it talked to them. For the most part they do not use metaphorical language. With children, what they see is what you get.

Notice that in this young boy's story, he talks about spending time with a *lady.* He clearly remembered seeing a woman and not a man, which suggests that he could tell the difference between the two, either in the soul's shape or in facial features. That he was later able to recognize a photograph of his grandmother as being the lady he saw is also significant—in this case, he remembered the appearance of the soul he had met and recognized it in the photograph, and not the other way around. So the boy saw something that he identified *visually* as a person; not only that, a person of a specific gender, and not only that but someone who turned out to be a specific person *whom he had never met.* That's a very specific kind of look for a soul, don't you think?

The Bible also has several interesting incidents that suggest that the soul has a recognizable form that looks a lot like our bodies. For example, the apostle Paul mentions a moment when he "was caught up to the third heaven. Whether it was in the body or out of the body I do not know" (2 Cor. 12:2 NIV). This sounds to me like he couldn't tell the difference between the body and the soul because the two looked and felt exactly alike.

In the Gospel of Matthew, we find an incident where Jesus took several disciples with him to the top of Mount Tabor, a high hill in the middle of Galilee. There, two people suddenly appeared to speak with Jesus.

> After six days Jesus took with him Peter, James and John the brother of James, and led them up a high mountain by themselves. There he was transfigured before them. His face shone like the sun, and his clothes became as white as the light. Just then there appeared before them Moses and Elijah, talking with Jesus. Peter said to Jesus, "Lord, it is good for us to be here. If you wish, I will put up three shelters—one for you, one for Moses and one for Elijah." (Matt. 17:1–4 NIV)

What happened here? The disciples immediately recognized these spirits as Moses and Elijah even though clearly Peter and the rest had never met either one. I can't speculate as to why that would be possible, but I'm pretty certain they weren't wearing name tags. There must be something about our souls that makes us readily recognizable to anyone as individuals—and not just any individuals, but the unique individuals that are "us."

The Soul Appears to Resemble the Earthly Body

Notice how at Mount Tabor, Peter suggests building shelters for Moses and Elijah—perhaps to protect them from the weather. (I love Peter, always ready to do the wrong thing for the right reason.) Now let's think about that for a moment. Do you recognize a nebulous blob of light as a hero of the faith? Do you assume a cloud of pretty colors needs shelter from sun, wind, and rain? I don't think so. I think Peter and the others saw the two spirits as people—heads, hands, bodies, feet, the whole shebang. And Peter, grasping for what to do in the midst of this incredible event, settled on the one thing he knew that a person appreciates in a hot, sunny climate: a nice, shady gazebo to sit under. Why? Because our souls look a lot like our bodies.

So if our souls have bodies that look like our own, will those bodies be fat or thin, young or old, plain or handsome? I can only say that our souls—our spiritual bodies—will look like ourselves. (Maybe I should lose a few pounds now, just in case.) Fortunately, according to the Bible, God offers to make our spiritual bodies perfect—he "will transform our lowly bodies so that they will be like his glorious body" (Phil. 3:21 NIV). That's an offer I think I'll accept—how about you?

So now you have to make a judgment based on the evidence. Does the soul exist or not? I think the evidence weighs more heavily in favor of the soul than against it. I'm willing to base my faith on that. Are you?

So if there is a soul, why does it exist? What is its purpose, and where does it come from?

PART III

God: Does He Exist?

CHAPTER 8

God or No God?

NOT LONG AGO, my staff and I decided to address the question: Does God exist? We realized, however, that if we used that question as the series title people would have one of three reactions: They might just answer the question yes and not bother to hear what we had to say. They might answer the question no and not bother to hear what we had to say. Or they might answer the question, "I don't know and don't care" and not bother to hear what we had to say. The last thing we wanted was a collective shrug.

So we decided to bypass that with a title that we knew would generate interest—we called it "The Ignorance of Atheism." We did a big marketing blitz using this title. We sent mailers to people's homes and designed a billboard with a huge monkey on it and placed it on the major road that runs near our church.

The title worked. Nobody who saw it just shrugged. Everyone was curious about how we could make such a bold statement. Several irate atheists called us to complain: "How dare you call me ignorant?" And we just politely urged them to come hear what we had to say. And they did, many with open minds.

An Ignorant Philosophy

Yes, it is a provocative claim, and one I stand by. But I don't make that claim to call atheists ignorant. I do it to call the *philosophy* of atheism ignorant. In fact, I borrowed that approach from two of the leading proponents of atheism in the world today, professor Richard Dawkins and journalist Christopher Hitchens.

In his book *God Is Not Great,* Christopher Hitchens says, "Religion poisons everything." His book includes the following chapter titles:

> Chapter Two: Religion Kills
> Chapter Four: A Note on Health, to Which Religion Can Be Hazardous
> Chapter Eight: The "New" Testament Exceeds the Evil of the "Old" One
> Chapter Sixteen: Is Religion Child Abuse? (In which he basically says "Yes, it is.")[1]

Or consider Professor Dawkins, who titled one of his books *The God Delusion* and says religion is like "a child with a dummy in its mouth. I do not think it a very dignified or respect-worthy posture for an adult to go around sucking a dummy for comfort."[2] (*Dummy* is a British word for what Americans call an infant pacifier.)

Provocative statements, don't you think? If you happen to be a religious person, you might feel offended. These quotes seem to say that if you are religious and share your faith, you are poisoning people. They seem to say you are unhealthy. They seem to say that if you share the teachings of the Bible with someone, you are a pusher of evil. And if you teach your child any sort of religion, you are guilty of child abuse. As if those words are not bad enough, they seem to say that if you are a Christian, then you are deluded and ignorant. Just like those atheists who called our church, you might be tempted to shout, "How dare you call me ignorant? How dare you call me a child abuser? How dare you call me evil?"

But you would be assuming these very things unjustly, because you would be interpreting something personally that is not being applied to you. Neither Hitchens nor Dawkins is attacking religious *people.* They are attacking *religion.* Theirs is not a personal battle, but rather a philosophical one.

I am doing the same thing when I call atheism "ignorant." I am saying that it is the *philosophy* of atheism that is ignorant, not those who follow it. A person who is very well-informed about atheism is not an ignorant person. If a person knows about all the underlying concepts, ideas, and themes that seem to support atheism, that person would clearly not be ignorant of those things. But that doesn't mean that those positions themselves are not ignorant or based on false information.

So when I say that atheism is ignorant, I am placing myself squarely in the philosophical debate with Dawkins and Hitchens—we just happen to be on opposite teams.

Doubt and Understanding

Many Christians and even many ministers do not like to engage in this debate. They would rather shout the atheists down, ignore their questions, demand that no one ever ask such questions—or worse, condemn someone who asks questions.

I believe that attitude is very wrong. No one should ever be afraid of questions, least of all difficult ones. It is only by facing such questions that we can actually find answers. It is okay to raise doubts because that is how you come to understanding. Doubt doesn't weaken understanding; instead, doubt, properly examined, *strengthens* understanding.

Some people argue that religion teaches us to be satisfied with not understanding. While that may be true of some religions, that is certainly not true of Christianity. Jesus himself said, "Keep on asking and keep on seeking and keep on knocking" (Luke 11:9, my paraphrase). You cannot seek without asking questions. You cannot find without discovering answers.

Real Faith Comes from Evidence

You've probably heard the argument that faith is blind and there can be no rationale behind it. I beg to differ. Faith is only blind when there is no evidence for it. If I believe that a space alien is going to hover over my house in a flying saucer and give me cosmic honey buns, that would be blind faith, because there is no evidence to support it. *That* would be faith based on nonsense, and it would be baloney.

But real faith isn't based on nonsense. Real faith is based on evidence.

Evidence, Not Proof

Unfortunately, believers and nonbelievers alike misunderstand what that means. They assume that evidence can only be rock-solid proof. But faith and proof are incompatible. If you have proof for something, you don't need faith. If I believe that if I drop a rock it will hit the ground, that's not faith. It's not even belief. It's just knowledge. Faith is different. Faith is what happens when you sit in a chair you've never seen before. You expect that chair to support your weight. But you don't actually know that it will. Yes, you've probably sat in other chairs. You've probably seen people sitting in similar chairs. And you know that chairs are intended to support your weight. But none of that is *proof.* It's just evidence. Only after you have trusted that chair with your weight do you have proof. Proof may follow faith, but faith is not based on proof.

The Bible links faith and evidence: "Now faith is the substance of things hoped for, the evidence of things not seen" (Heb. 11:1 NKJV).

I cannot provide you with proof of anything. Not the soul, not the afterlife, not heaven, not hell, and not God. The truth is, no one can do that. Nor can any person prove the opposite point of view. Whether someone believes there is a God or there is not a God is solely a decision of faith. But remember, either way, faith should not be blind. It should be reasonable and rational. It should be based on evidence. The problem is that not many people have really looked at the evidence.

Is There Evidence for God?

I've had many conversations with people who profess atheism. Most try to argue their positions with some statement of "proof." Only it is never actually proof at all. It's merely evidence they have chosen to interpret in favor of the belief they already hold (or at least want to be true) that there is no God.

One conversation happened at the end of our series. An atheist who had come to listen asked to speak with me after one of our services. He told me he still wasn't convinced by what I had to say. I agreed to listen to his thoughts, and he began by saying, "You're basing a lot of your belief that God exists on your understanding of the Bible, aren't you?"

I nodded and said, "Yes, I would say that would be a pretty fair statement."

He crossed his arms and said, "Well, it's pretty obvious that the Bible cannot be trusted, that it's not reliable."

"Why is that?" I asked.

He said, "Well, for one thing, would you agree that sex should only be enjoyed within the confines of marriage?"

I had to agree that the Bible teaches that.

"If that's the case," he replied, "then why is it that people like me have a continual urge to have sex when we're not married? Why would we have such an urge like that if sex was created by God to only be experienced within the confines of marriage?"

This was his argument. But I think you can see what I saw—that it wasn't actually proof of anything at all in regard to the existence of God. Rather, the man's statement said more about him than about God. And that was my reply: "You're not actually weighing the evidence for or against God. You just don't want to put your faith in him because then you wouldn't be able to have sex outside of marriage."

The man didn't want to be forced, if you will, to change his behavior. He knew that if the God of the Bible existed, then he would be disobedient to God, and that would produce a hypocrisy within himself he didn't want to face. So his reasoning for believing God didn't exist wasn't based on the evidence. It was based on his own particular behavior that he didn't want to change.

A second man came to me claiming that he had proof that atheism was true. He had formerly been a devout Christian but had abandoned his faith based on this proof, so naturally I was curious to hear what had provoked such a profound change. The proof, he said, was in a particular species of monkeys.

"Monkeys?" I said. I was at this point expecting some argument based on Darwinism and a missing link.

"Yes. These monkeys practice homosexuality."

Well, that was a new one on me. I had to give him credit for originality.

He continued, "It is perfectly natural for them. And since they practice homosexuality, there must not be a God."

If you're having a hard time following the logic here, you can imagine how I felt sitting across from this man. "Okay," I replied, "what's your point?"

"If the Bible is true and God made us all, then none of us should have homosexual tendencies. I suppose you could reason why they exist in human beings capable of free will, but how do you explain these tendencies in animals that don't have an innate sense on the inside? That is proof that God does not exist."

"Let me get this straight. You say this one species of monkeys naturally practices homosexuality, out of all the millions of species of animals that exist on this planet, and that is your proof that God does not exist?"

"Yes," he replied. And no, he wasn't trying to pull a joke.

"This is your best evidence?" I said. I wanted to give him a chance for something better. "Are you certain you don't want to pick something else?"

He said he was certain. He'd stick with the monkeys.

"Well, then," I said, "I really even hate to respond to you, because in general I believe the Christian church has been very ugly to those who practice homosexuality, and I don't want to pile on. But for the sake of our conversation, I will indulge you. How many animal species do you think exist on this planet?"

"I don't know," he said.

"I don't know, either. But let's assume it's as low as ten thousand. What you're saying is that in one out of all ten thousand species we see evidence of homosexual behavior. But in 9,999 species we see a tendency for heterosexual behavior. So if we were to look at the total evidence, we would assume that God's preference is clearly for heterosexual behavior. To draw a conclusion from one of ten thousand would be a bad conclusion, because it isn't based on the evidence. So if you're not drawing your conclusion based on the evidence, you're drawing it based on something else."

And that in fact was the case. This man, as it turns out, was married to a devout Christian woman but had decided he wanted out of the marriage. He had rationalized that if he no longer believed in God, she would grant him a divorce. Because he wanted a "morally acceptable" path out of the marriage, he sought "proof" that God does not exist. And so he chose monkeys—creatures with no moral code to begin with—as his "proof," arguing that since God didn't make monkeys to abide by the moral expectations for humans, those moral expectations were invalid, and therefore God did not exist. But he didn't have "proof" at all—he merely had one bit of evidence that he interpreted in favor of a viewpoint he wanted to be true in order to justify his own wishes. Sadly, he clung to his "proof" through the rest of our talk. (By the way, I am not trying to debate the morality of homosexuality one way or the other. I am simply pointing out the flaw in this man's reasoning.)

My third conversation revolved around a much more classical argument. In this case the atheist posed the following question:

"If an all-loving God exists, then how does he allow all this pain and sorrow in the world? The two are contradictory. I don't believe God exists because of all the pain and sorrow."

I replied, "Well, first of all that's a faulty conclusion. The proper conclusion would be 'I don't believe he's a good and loving God,' not that he doesn't exist. So your argument really is not that he doesn't exist, it's just that he's cruel. But I'll allow for your view for the sake of conversation. So I'll agree with you that God doesn't exist."

At that point my visitor looked at me strangely. Obviously, it had caught him off guard to hear a minister make such a statement.

"But I have a question for you," I continued. "Since we both agree that God doesn't exist, my question is: Are there still pain and suffering in the world?"

He said, "Well, yes."

"So, if there are still pain and suffering in the world and God doesn't exist, then God can't be responsible for the pain and suffering, can he?"

And the atheist agreed that had to be true.

"Then where do the pain and suffering come from?"

He thought about my question for a moment. "Obviously, they come from the choices of mankind."

"Exactly. So now that we both know that pain and suffering can't come from God but must come from man, can we bring God back into the picture?"

Now I don't offer these stories as contradictions of all atheist arguments. Clearly, as evangelists for atheism, my three visitors were amateurs. But I do offer these stories as cautionary tales against grabbing any piece of evidence and offering it as unquestionable proof of your faith—and that's advice believers ought to follow as well.

So as I offer evidence for God, remember that what I am offering is *evidence,* not proof. Just as a juror must weigh the evidence presented in court and decide whether it favors guilt or innocence, you must do the same with the evidence I present: Does it favor the existence of God or not?

Also obviously, I am a Christian. My faith is in the God of the Bible, the Old Testament and the New. However, in this chapter I am not arguing that you must believe in that God, much less the traditional representations of that God in art or literature or even Christian theology. I am merely putting forth the possibility that a God does indeed exist, and then examining the nature of what that God must be like, given the evidence we have. So if you do not believe in God, I want you to consider, like the men in my stories, *why* you have chosen not to do so. Is it because you assume there are moral implications that would cast your own life in a poor light? Or have you met people who claim to be Christians who have treated you poorly or presented a God to you that you find distasteful? Or do you have emotional or even moral arguments based on history or natural events that make you dislike religion or for which you would put blame on God?

If your answer to any of these is yes, remember, then, that you are not actually operating on evidence but on personal preference. The real question is not whether you approve of God or not, but whether God exists. Not wanting God to exist is not proof, nor is it evidence. And wanting God to exist is not proof or evidence, either. So both of us need to agree to look at the evidence with an open mind. After that, we can deal with faith.

CHAPTER 9

Big Bang or Intelligent Designer?

IN CONSIDERING HOW the world was derived, there are at least a couple of philosophies to examine.

THE TELEOLOGICAL ARGUMENT: A BRAIN BEHIND IT ALL

Let's start with the first bit of evidence, which is known in philosophical circles as the *teleological argument. Teleological* is a big word, and I know it doesn't pop up in everyday speech. It means "the logical end" or "the purpose" of a thing. This argument basically says that any reasonable person, when examining or discovering a thing of sophisticated complexity, concludes that there was an intelligent designer behind it. After all, isn't this the conclusion we always come to when examining sophisticated and complex things?

Consider the following.

The Round Rock Example

Imagine you enter a cave and find a pile of tiny rocks shaped as perfect spheres with holes through the exact center of each. Do you say, "Oh, look how the natural geological processes created these perfectly spherical rocks with perfectly straight holes in them"? No, of course not. Geologic processes are never that precise. Instead, you recognize that these rocks are man-made beads. You know they are the product of deliberate, intelligent design. That they could occur naturally is so unlikely as to be impossible. The very existence of those beads is evidence that somebody made them. If an object is complex, precise, and logical, then it is reasonable to assume it had an intelligent creator.

The Alien Inscription Example

Imagine an astronaut walks into a cave on Mars and discovers a series of scratches that coincide with the first one hundred prime numbers in sequence. Wouldn't he immediately conclude those markings were left by an intelligent being? Wouldn't he conclude that ET had engaged in a little mathematical graffiti?

So if a message is complex and logical, then it is reasonable to assume it had an intelligent source.

The Automobile Example

Open the hood of your car and look at the engine system, with all its wires, belts, hoses, pipes, connectors, and other devices. After looking at it, would you conclude it was the result of a random explosion in a metal factory? Of course not! Even if you had never seen any such thing as an automobile engine before, you would guess that an intelligent someone had designed it and put it all together.

The City Example

Imagine you are someone raised solely in the country, and one day you encounter a city with all its buildings and houses. Even if you had never seen a city before, if someone asked you "How did it get here?" you would never explain it as the result of a big storm in the woods. No, you would reply that obviously somebody intelligent designed and built it all.

So the fact is that it's very logical, when you look at something complex and sophisticated, to assume that there is somebody intelligent behind it.

The Atheist Argument: The Uncaused Explosion

Atheism will tell us that this highly complex world is the result of a random, uncaused explosion that just happened to produce the sophistication and complexity that we find in our universe. Personally, I have a hard time believing that an explosion could create that type of order. If you throw a stick of dynamite in a house, the house is not going to blow up and have all the pieces fall down in a sequence. They're not going to fall in size order. You're not going to see all the red things fall in one spot, all the blue things fall in another spot, and all the green things in another spot. They're going to be chaotically mixed up. We all know this instinctively. When I see the mess my son has made of his room each week, I may say, "It looks like a bomb went off in here!" Maybe you've said the same thing yourself. We say that because we *know* that explosions create great disorder. They scatter things about, flinging them willy-nilly, in completely random ways.

But it's not just explosions that do this. All nature does this. You've seen pictures of the devastation from disasters around the world: the tsunamis that hit Indonesia and Japan, the floods along the Mississippi, the tornadoes that tore through Alabama and Missouri. Was anything in their wake left in a state of order? Hardly. Even on a small scale, we know this is true. If you leave a car outside for several years and don't do anything to it, you're going to come back and find out that it won't work. Parts will have corroded or frozen up or become brittle. On their own, things just break down, don't they? Of course they do. And it takes a lot of deliberate effort to set them right again.

Scientists even have a term for this phenomenon: the *law of entropy.* The law of entropy states that highly ordered systems move toward disorder—just like a kid's room or an old car—and only become ordered through the direct input of energy. Scientific observation teaches us that disordered systems *never* become more ordered on their own. Yet atheism would have us believe that the most disordered event we can imagine—a huge explosion—produced a universe of incredibly intricate and detailed order, with no outside input at all. How can that be?

Paul C. W. Davies, professor at Arizona State University, theoretical physicist, cosmologist, and astrobiologist, has said, "Through my scientific study I have come to believe more and more strongly that the physical universe is put together with an ingenuity so astonishing that I cannot accept it merely as a brute fact." As a young man Davies had stated his position as an agnostic—that is, someone who believes the question about the existence of God is unanswerable—but due to his scientific studies, he has concluded that a Creator must exist.[1]

Fred Hoyle was the physicist who coined the phrase "the Big Bang" (though he actually disagreed with the theory). When researching the phenomenally precise and detailed requirements for the formation of life, he concluded, "A common sense interpretation of the facts suggests a super intellect has monkeyed with physics, as well as with chemistry and biology, and that there are no blind forces worth speaking about in nature. The numbers one calculates from the facts seem to me so overwhelming as to put this conclusion almost beyond question."[2]

When you look at the sophisticated complexity of the universe and all the things in it, a fair, honest, and intelligent conclusion is that it is highly improbable that it happened by chance or was always just there. Rather, the universe is the creation of some intelligent being that is uncaused—namely, God.

Those physicists are merely recognizing the truth of what King David wrote thousands of years ago: "The heavens declare the glory of God; the skies proclaim the work of his hands" (Ps. 19:1 NIV).

The Evidence of Man

But if you think the heavens are complex and sophisticated, wait until we look at the most sophisticated and complex thing of all—man. If you need evidence of God, you need only glance in a mirror. You are an incredibly complex device consisting of countless parts, all performing intricate functions with an accuracy and precision that mankind has yet to duplicate. Is there a camera as versatile as the human eye? Are there artificial limbs as nimble or responsive as the human leg? Is there a computer as imaginative as the human brain? No on all counts.

Is it any wonder why the Bible says, "What is mankind that you are mindful of them, human beings that you care for them? You have made them a little lower than the angels and crowned them with glory and honor"? (Ps. 8:4–5 NIV).

Another psalm continues this thought, saying, "Oh, yes, you shaped me first inside, then out; you formed me in my mother's womb. I thank you, High God—you're breathtaking! Body and soul, I am marvelously made! I worship in adoration—what a creation! You know me inside and out, you know every bone in my body; you know exactly how I was made, bit by bit, how I was sculpted from nothing into something" (Ps. 139:13–16 *The Message*).

When we examine the complexity and sophistication of our own bodies, I believe, we must consider that as evidence of an intelligent designer, just as we would any other complex device. Being "natural" does not deny the possibility of an intelligent designer; it just denies the possibility of a merely human one. Nature doesn't deny God; nature merely reveals his power.

CHAPTER 10

Who Made God?

THE NEXT IMPORTANT evidence we should consider begins with the idea of *contingent things and events*. You might also call it "something comes from something." We are all innately aware of this concept. When we see an object or an event, we automatically know that it didn't just appear out of nowhere. Consider a book (maybe this one). You know that it didn't just pop into being. You know that the existence of a book is *contingent* upon many other things existing and happening. The book is made of paper and ink, which are made from trees and chemicals, which are produced by people who gather and shape these things. The words come from a writer, who is helped by a number of people—editors, agents, proofreaders, and so on. If all of these things and people did not exist, doing all the things they do, then the book could not exist. It is *contingent* upon all those things.

In fact, we know that *everything* we interact with in our universe is contingent upon other things. This is made of that, that is caused by this.

So the question becomes: Is the universe itself a contingent thing? And if it is, on what is it contingent?

Most reasonable people would assume that there are only two explanations for the universe and the world we live in:

1. It's always existed. (It is *not* contingent.)
2. It was created or caused by someone or something. (It *is* contingent.)

So the question before us is: Which is more reasonable? And I stress the word *reasonable* as opposed to *provable,* because neither is provable. We are not interested in proof; we are interested in faith, which is based on reasonable evidence, not proof.

The Universe and the Second Law of Thermodynamics

Well, let's start with the universe: Is it reasonable to assume that it always existed? The answer is no. Why? Because of what's known as the *second law of thermodynamics.*

The second law of thermodynamics is directly related to our old friend, the law of entropy (they are essentially one and the same). According to the second law of thermodynamics, energy only moves in one direction—that is, from a state of high energy to a state of lesser energy. In other words, like a car burning all the gasoline in its tank, the energy always runs out. You can't reverse the car engine and put the gasoline back.

Well, our universe is like a big car engine. It is running out of energy. But even more than that, the law of entropy states that as our universe gives up its energy, it decays. And anything that is decaying or deteriorating will eventually come to an end. Only unlike for a car, there won't be any gasoline for a fill-up. When the universe runs out of energy, everything stops. Period. This is just a brute fact. Just like you and me, the universe will die. (Kind of spoils the dreams of all those people wanting a medical solution for mortality. There can't be any immortality in this universe because one day it's all going to end. So even if doctors do "cure" aging, you will still eventually die, one way or another.)

But isn't it also a brute fact that anything that has an end must have had a beginning? Doesn't all the evidence we see around us point to that fact? You cannot name one thing on this world or any other (or even outside this world) that did not have a beginning and does not have an end. Even the stars have birthdays—

and even the stars eventually die. So all the evidence says that anything that has an end had a beginning. Therefore, it stands to reason that the universe, which is headed toward an end, must have had a beginning.

And if it had a beginning, must it not have had a beginner? (Or, as scientists put it, a *first cause.*)

Now I know that atheism argues that all of this is possible because there are many universes happening over and over, all at the same time, so naturally one was bound to hit it right once. (You know what they call people who bet that way at a casino? Broke.) But where is the evidence for this concept of multiple universes? The truth is, there isn't any. In *Scientific American,* cosmologist George F. R. Ellis cautions his colleagues about the lack of evidence for the idea. "The case for the multiverse is inconclusive... it is more a concept than a well-defined theory." In the same article, he admits, "The universe might be pure happenstance. . . . Or things might in some sense be meant to be the way they are—purpose or intent somehow underlies existence. Science cannot determine which is the case." His article concludes, "Nothing is wrong with scientifically based philosophical speculation, which is what multiverse proposals are. But we should name it for what it is."[1]

Atheism may claim there are randomly occurring universes, but the actual scientific evidence does not support that claim (talk about blind faith!). If anything, the physical, provable facts point only to one universe, ever. So the actual evidence would indicate that the universe is a deliberate creation rather than a random accident.

So not only do we have a beginning, we have a deliberate beginning, and a deliberate beginner. Our first cause has become a first causer.

"But what causes the first cause?" asks atheism, thinking it has caught the evidence in a quandary of unending causes. But that's where atheism again runs into the evidence. The answer is, "Nothing; the first cause is eternal, and needs no cause." But if the universe is contingent, you ask, how can this be? The answer is that time, entropy, cause and effect, and so forth are all properties *of* the universe—that is, they are inherent to it and everything within it (including you and me). But that doesn't mean that any of these things are properties of whatever might be external to the universe.

Think of the universe as your house. What are the properties of a house? Well, it has walls, a roof, doors, windows, maybe a temperature-control system, maybe furniture. So, then, are all these things properties of the world outside your house? No, of course not. You know for a fact that the world actually has none of those properties! The world has no roof. The world has no walls. The world has no doors, no windows, no temperature-control system, and no furniture. The world has rain, wind, freezing winter temperatures, blazing summer heat, hard ground, and lots of lumpy rocks and roots (which you know if you've ever been camping in a tent). In fact, because the world has none of the comfortable qualities of a house, we build houses to create a more livable environment for us. So it is the world outside the house that dictates what the properties of the house are, not the other way around.

In the same way, whatever is external to the universe does not share the same properties of the universe. The first cause can contain those properties and even dictates that they exist within the universe, but it is not subject to those same rules itself. It is not contingent or decaying or defined by time or cause and effect at all. It is outside these properties altogether. The first cause does not need the universe or any of the universe's properties in order to exist or maintain its own existence any more than nature needs houses.

Now given all of the above, let's consider what is reasonable to assume about the cause of the universe's beginning. Would it not have the following characteristics?

- uncaused by anything else
- totally self-reliant and self-sufficient
- unaffected by time, with neither beginning nor end

You could sum it all up by saying, "Almighty, all-powerful, and eternal." Sounds like God to me.

Is it any coincidence, then, that the Bible describes God in the same terms?

> "The eternal God is thy refuge." (Deut. 33:27 KJV)

> Your throne was established long ago; you are from all eternity. (Ps. 93:2 NIV)

> "I am the Alpha and the Omega, the Beginning and the End." (Rev. 21:6 NIV)

The Bible's name for God is of interesting note. Unlike all other faiths, which give their gods names without meaning, or names that are descriptive nouns, the Hebrew name for God is a verb—a verb of being. More than that, it is a sentence—in English it translates as the first person singular, present tense statement of being: "I Am." Not "I Was." Not "I Will Be." But simply and definitely, "I Am" (Exod. 3:14). It is a statement of ultimate being—an entity that (unlike all other gods) has no origin and no end. A being that is eternal, self-reliant, self-sufficient, and uncaused. The very sort of being the cosmological evidence leads us to assume must exist in order for the universe to exist.

I Am.

The noncontingent being.

The first cause.

God.

CHAPTER 11

My Right, Your Wrong

AT THIS POINT, we've examined sufficient scientific evidence to come to a rational conclusion that God exists. It certainly seems more rational than the conclusion that a universe that is clearly coming to an end instead always was, or had no external cause.

But the evidence doesn't end there. We have evidence not only in our world, but also in ourselves.

Consider this incident that exhibits what I call "the jerk factor": my wife and I were at the airport on our way to Dallas, Texas, to speak on the *Praise the Lord* television show. As we were on a deadline, I requested that the check-in person move us to the front of the plane so we could exit quickly. While she was checking for availability, I heard this commotion going on behind me. I looked around to see a long line of people forming to check in. There was only one problem: one particular family had decided to go sit on the benches about a hundred feet from the line and had left their baggage (twelve pieces of big, bright red luggage) blocking the entrance to the line. An airport worker recognized the obstruction and decided to move the luggage out of the way. When he did, out of nowhere a little guy charged right up to the airport worker and started yelling. "Why are you touching my luggage? Don't you know you're not supposed to touch anyone's luggage? Leave my luggage alone!" He was going on and on and on and he wouldn't stop.

At that point another man stepped in. He was huge—six-six

and about four hundred pounds; you would not want to mess with this guy. He walked up to the little screaming guy—who was five-two and maybe a hundred forty on a rainy day—and said, "You are a jerk."

Now I'm not an expert at predicting outcomes, but if I had tried to predict who would win in a fight between the two, I would have chosen the big guy, hands down. If I had been the little guy, I would have sized things up and walked away. But that's not what this little guy did. Instead, he ran right up to the big guy and shoved his face right in the big guy's stomach. (I thought, *Is he getting any air? Is he going to make it out alive?*) And then the little guy screamed, "I'm a jerk? I'm a jerk? No, you're a jerk!"

The point of this story is what compelled the little guy to react as he did. The argument between the big guy and the little guy centered around *expected* behavior. Notice that neither man said that the other's behavior displeased him personally (even if it did). Instead, each implied that there was a universal code that was independent of what they individually liked. "You're a jerk" does not mean "You are behaving in a way I personally dislike." It means "You are violating a code of behavior, which means you are 'being a jerk.'"

When people argue, they invariably do so based on a mutual assumption that a code of behavior exists that we all know instinctively. If I say that something isn't fair, you are more than likely going to interpret what I have said according to a standard of fairness; you are not likely to reject the concept that something *can* be fair.

That's how we think: we are more likely to agree that a standard exists, so that the fight is over interpretation, rather than to reject the standard outright. The little guy didn't question that there was a code that could define someone as being a jerk; he just applied it to the big guy and assumed it didn't apply to him.

That, too, is typical of human behavior. Nearly always, the person being accused of violating the code tries to defend why he or she *didn't* violate it, or claims a special set of circumstances that lets them off the hook in that particular instance. Think about people who illegally download music and movies off the Internet. All of those people would agree that there is such a thing as stealing and that stealing is wrong (just try walking away with their iPods and see how they react). When they defend their illegal activity, they don't argue that stealing isn't wrong—they just claim that in their cases they aren't stealing. So we still agree that some sort of standard of right and wrong exists, as much as we try to weasel our way out of it when we cross the line.

The Source of the Standard

So where does this code come from? Well, there are certain things about this code of right or wrong that are strikingly observable.

1. This Code Seems to Cross Cultures and Civilizations

Sure, there are some differences, but nothing that really amounts to anything like a total difference. Nearly all cultures throughout history emphasize the importance of kindness, honesty, loyalty, and love, and condemn cruelty, deceit, betrayal, and hate.

That doesn't mean that people, even whole cultures, don't violate the code. But in order to violate it, they nearly always come up with some justification for why they aren't violating it or why it doesn't apply in their particular circumstances. Even the most virulent racist basically argues that it's okay for him to violate the code of right and wrong against people of another race, not because no code exists, but because he believes the code doesn't apply to the target of his hate. He believes in the code; he just excuses his actions from it.

So even when you allow for justification, when you examine this code of right and wrong, it seems to be universally present in every human being.

2. This Code Seems to Be More Than Mere Instinct or Personal Preference

One night, at about two thirty in the morning, my house alarm went off. If you've never been wakened in the middle of the night by a security alarm, I can assure you that it's a very unnerving experience. I woke up wondering what was going on and what to do about it. Next to my bed there is a keypad that tells me what has triggered the alarm. I looked at the keypad, and it indicated the front door had been opened. Now I was really unnerved. Someone or something had opened my front door? Were they in our house?

That particular night we had held a family movie night with the kids in our bedroom, and everyone had fallen asleep in our big master bed. So the kids were there with Lisa and me, and I knew we were all together and safe for the moment. But I didn't know what was happening outside our bedroom. My natural instinct at that point was to protect my family, but also to figure out what had set off the alarm. My mind began to race, telling me that someone was in our house and that we had to avoid the danger.

Outside my bedroom is a balcony from which I knew I could see the front door. I slipped through the bedroom door as quietly as I could and looked down to see the front door was indeed open—not just gapped, but wide-open, as if somebody had just walked through and not bothered to close it at all. At this point I was totally freaked out. I grabbed a baseball bat that I keep under my bed, and being the manly man that I am, I said to Lisa, "Why don't you come with me?"

She replied, "I'm not coming with you! You go check it out by yourself!"

I suppose it was good to have my role as protector of the family confirmed, although at the time I felt more like the sacrificial lamb—especially when Lisa locked the bedroom door behind me!

But bat in hand, I performed my duty and searched the house, ready to scream like crazy when I came upon the intruder. (I have no idea what else I would have done, but I'm pretty sure that screaming would have been involved.)

To my relief there was no intruder. It turned out the kids hadn't closed the door completely when they came in for dinner that evening, and the wind had blown it open, triggering the alarm. But I didn't know any of that when I stepped out of my bedroom and let Lisa lock herself and the kids inside. Now I had wanted my wife to come with me for safety. That was my instinct—safety in numbers. Yet I knew that it was the right thing to do for me to brave the danger alone while she and the kids stayed behind that locked door.

How did I know that?

Because the code of right and wrong is more than instinct or personal preference.

But you may say, "Well, of course you would risk yourself for your family, Frank." True. But what about situations where people accept great danger to themselves despite having no personal connection at all with others?

I vividly recall the moment I learned about the attack on the World Trade Center in New York City on September 11, 2001. I remember seeing the dreadful fires on television, and watching in horror as the first tower seemed to peel apart like a banana. Everywhere the cameras turned, people were rushing away from the towers, trying to save themselves.

But not all of them. There were men and women that day who headed into the towers, climbing the stairs to help others get out. Some were policemen, some were firefighters, some were just regular people trying to help. Every desire of their hearts must have been to see loved ones again. Every instinct of their beings had to have been screaming, "Get out! Run! Avoid the danger!" Yet they did not. Why? Because they knew that going against that instinct to try and help others was the right thing to do.

This code of right and wrong is more than mere instinct or personal preference.

3. *This Code Seems to Help Us Determine When a Natural Instinct Is Good or Bad*

Consider instincts that we all have: the sexual instinct and the killer instinct.

There is nothing wrong with the natural instinct to want to have sex. Not only is it pleasurable, it's how we procreate, both of which are good things. However, our innate code seems to tell us that if you are married and you have sex outside of that marriage, it's wrong. If you don't believe that, ask yourself how many people are likely to brag about adultery to their spouses—or especially to their children. Can you imagine it? "What did you do today, dear?" "Oh, I had really great sex with somebody from Accounting. How was your day, honey?"

Let's say someone you knew bragged about how much she cheated on her husband; what would you think of that person? Would you think of her behavior as good, neutral, or wrong?

Even the media that tries to sell us on the idea that promiscuity is okay can't wait to expose and ridicule the behavior of celebrities caught in the act. Why? Because even they know it's wrong, and they know we do, too. If you question that standard, consider this: what do we see as the symbol of a sex life richly lived? An old man dying alone and unmourned after a past of constant infidelity? Or an elderly couple walking side by side and hand in hand after a lifetime of faithful commitment? Which would you choose for yourself?

Another instinct we have is the killer instinct. Yes, this exists. When people are pushed emotionally or physically, they will kill. We see it all too often in the world. But we also have an inherent rejection of killing, too. A study of soldiers in World War II discovered that most would refuse to fire a weapon at another human being, at a rate of almost 80 percent. Some soldiers reported being surprised to find that even after an intense battle, in which they recall aiming at multiple enemy soldiers, they hadn't used any of their ammunition. They intended to kill, but their fingers wouldn't pull the triggers—and they never noticed.[1]

Why is that? Because we know—we all know—that murder is wrong. So not only do we have an instinct to kill, we have an instinct not to.

But there are also other standards that come in with regard to the killer instinct. Just as we know we must overcome our instinct to kill when we are angered or stressed, we also know that we must overcome our instinct *not* to kill when failure to do so would cause more grievous harm—for example, when a police officer comes upon an armed robber or rapist, or if children are threatened, or in self-defense, or if we are soldiers acting in war. Our code teaches us that if we kill someone under these circumstances, we have not committed murder, but if we kill someone just because we are angry or do not like them, we have. And we know that if we fail to kill someone we know is threatening great harm, such as a suicide bomber headed toward a crowded city square, *we* would be as wrong as they are.

So we have a code that helps us determine when a natural instinct is good or bad.

Let's examine this strange moral code again:

- This code seems to cross cultures and civilizations.
- This code seems to be more than mere instinct or personal preference.
- This code seems to help us determine when a natural instinct is good or bad.

Doesn't the evidence suggest that mankind has a strict moral law that has been built into each and every person? There's a reason that murders, thefts, rapes, and infidelities are front-page news while weddings, fiftieth anniversaries, births, and natural deaths are buried in the back of the paper. It's because breaking the moral law is more shocking to us than keeping it.

It's a Man Thing

Consider also that this code clearly does *not* exist in animals. When a shark attacks a seal, we say the shark has killed the seal, but we don't think the shark has murdered it. If your dog snatches a bone from another dog, you may yell "No!" at your dog, but you really don't expect it to understand the concept of theft or to feel guilty.

So animals do not have this innate moral law written on their hearts or consciences. Is a killer whale a murderer? No. Is a snake that swallows a bird's eggs a thief? No. Only man has this innate moral law. Of all the creatures, only man recognizes that might is not right, and that a moral code trumps natural instincts.

The Lawgiver

The fact that we do have this innate moral law written on our hearts is powerful evidence that there must have been a lawgiver who designed it into our fabric. The universe doesn't design such things. Nature doesn't design such things. Certainly "random accidents" don't design such things. All we have to do is look at the behavior of all the other creatures on earth to know they do not have the moral law that we do. All we have to do is look at the universe to see that it does not care what happens or who does something or why. And yet *we* do. Why? Because that moral code is indelibly written on our hearts, put there by a Creator who cares.[2]

Listen to how the apostle Paul expresses this truth:

> When outsiders who have never heard of God's law follow it more or less by instinct, they confirm its truth by their obedience. They show that God's law is not something alien, imposed on us from without, but woven into the very fabric of our creation. There is something deep within them that echoes God's yes and no, right and wrong. Their response to

> God's yes and no will become public knowledge on the day God makes his final decision about every man and woman. The Message from God that I proclaim through Jesus Christ takes into account all these differences. (Rom. 2:14–16 *The Message*)

The Amorality of Atheism

Remember the fellow who challenged the existence of God based on the existence of evil in the world? He was operating from a *moral code* that he expected God to follow, wasn't he? Look at the words of Hitchens that I shared earlier, that "religion kills" and that religion is a form of child abuse. Are these views not also based on some universal moral code that Hitchens believes in? The truth is that if you look at atheism, much of the criticism of religion is based *entirely* on moral grounds.

Well, then, where is that moral code coming from? If the atheistic belief system is true, there can be no innate moral standard. According to atheism, everything is just a random accident, including people. If that is true, then there can be no underlying moral standard that values the life of a person over that of a dog or a cat or even a bacterium. There can be no moral standard that says a person should behave one way and not another because the whole concept of "should" and "should not" cannot exist.

Instead, right and wrong must be distilled into personal preferences—what each person wants. The problem with that is that some people want to hurt others. That's how dictators like Adolf Hitler and Joseph Stalin justified their actions: what they wanted was the only thing that mattered because there was no God.

But with God suddenly everything matters. With God there can indeed be a moral standard—the very moral standard we so cherish, and which atheism itself puts forth. Why do we desire justice? Why do we value mercy? Why do we value loyalty and self-sacrifice? Why do we value compassion? There is no logical reason for atheism to put forth these concepts. They even fly in the face of our basic human desires—food, survival, sex. We can acquire all of these by acting in the most heinous manners imaginable—theft, murder, rape. Yet we know these acts are wrong, and not just wrong but evil. Why?

Atheism may argue that social values promote the furtherance of the species—but then, why should the individual care about that? What does a man care if he impregnates a woman and leaves her with yet another "random accident"? In a random world, does it matter to him that his DNA continues on? No, it doesn't. But let's presume that social values—in the formation of a tribe—can help an individual survive. What does that have to do with compassion? Why should a man in North America have compassion for a Japanese child orphaned by a tsunami? There is no social reason for it; in fact, if making certain one's own DNA survives is truly of instinctive importance, then the racists are correct, and people of other races should be eliminated to ensure that resources are limited to one's own tribe. Wasn't that the horrible, twisted argument of the Nazis, making sure their "tribe" came out on top? So if that child in Japan dies, what does the North American lose? In a random world, nothing. Instead, if *all* the children in Japan were to die, the man in North America stands to gain more resources for himself and his tribe from the lifeless island left behind.

But somehow we know that such selfish, tribal behavior is wrong. Despite the "evolutionary advantage" of "survival of the fittest" that atheism claims runs the world, in the long run we humans value the opposite approach. We believe in protecting the weak, limiting the powerful, punishing the greedy, aiding the injured, uplifting the fallen, and trying to make our world a better place for everyone else. Oh, yes, there are people who take the selfish route or the tribal route. But as a whole, we condemn such behavior, and certainly do not value it.

In fact, we have a word for people who decide moral standards do not apply, and everything comes down to doing whatever they want regardless of the consequences: *sociopath*. It's considered a mental disorder and turns up frequently among violent criminals. Not only do we know such behavior is inherently wrong, we believe it's a sign that a person has a mental illness. Why?

I think the evidence points to a knowledge that is placed in us by our Creator. I think that we, above all other creatures, were made to appreciate compassion, self-sacrifice, justice, mercy, generosity, loyalty, friendship, courage, honesty, honor, and love. I believe we know the difference between good and evil because there *is* a difference—and God has made that difference very clear to us in a way no random accident possibly could.

Tell me, which would you rather be the case: that there is a difference between good and evil, and that compassion, justice, mercy, love, and all the other virtues are real and expected of all mankind, or that there is no moral standard, and men can inflict as much harm and selfishness as they like without fear of punishment?

You get to choose. In one way lies heaven. And in the other lies hell. (And yes, we'll deal with both.)

So here is the evidence: Everything in the universe is contingent—caused by or dependent upon someone or something else for its creation and continued existence. Therefore everything in the universe had a beginning. Therefore it stands to reason that there must be a being who is noncontingent or uncaused, or self-sufficient or eternal or almighty (i.e., God), who caused or began the universe.

In the Beginning, God Created . . .

The complexity and sophistication of the universe in which we live and our very own complexity suggest beyond a reasonable doubt that there must be an intelligent designer beyond it all (i.e., God). This echoes the very first words of the Bible, "In the beginning, God created the heavens and the earth" (Gen. 1:1 NKJV).

The fact that all humanity is programmed with a strict moral code is evidence that there must have been a lawgiver who put it there (i.e., God). This, too, is echoed in Genesis when God declares his intent to make a creature like himself: "Then God said, 'Let Us make man in Our image, according to Our likeness'" (Gen. 1:26 NKJV).

So far, we've uncovered some powerful evidence that there is a God—certainly more than enough to put our faith in his existence. Yet there is one more bit of evidence that I'd like to add, and it is in the next chapter.

CHAPTER 12

Could So Many People Be Lying?

JUST AS ACROSS creeds and cultures humankind has a long history of believing in the existence of the soul, mankind also has a long history of believing in the existence of God. But more than that, there are millions of people who not only believe in God but also claim to have experienced a relationship with him. Granted, this argument in and of itself is far from conclusive, but it is nevertheless worthy of our consideration.

We all know that hundreds of millions of intelligent, well-adjusted people claim to have experienced the love of God. Atheism likes to pretend that all such people are, in the words of a recent atheist anthology, "unenlightened," "brainwashed," "stupid," "gullible," "uneducated," "deluded," "inferior," and "incompetent." (Lest I be accused of cherry-picking, these are among the least offensive descriptive terms the authors chose to use.)[1] In short, atheism looks upon believers as the intellectual great unwashed who simply don't know any better. But that's just pretense. Today you will find believers among all facets of humanity, from scientists to secretaries, from presidents to plumbers. Believers count among their ranks actors and astronauts, bankers and biologists, carpenters and cardiologists, doctors and dancers, engineers and educators, judges and janitors, philosophers and physicists—every respectable profession you can name.

These people are not deluded. These people are not ignorant.

These people are not uneducated and unsophisticated, or too lacking in intelligence to comprehend the lofty philosophical nuances of atheism. No, these people understand everything atheism expresses and collectively reject it as a failed philosophy. But that alone isn't the evidence. More than just having come to an intellectual knowledge of God, these people claim an *experiential* knowledge of God. They claim to experience the love of God. They claim to experience the forgiveness of God and the removal of guilt and shame for breaking his moral code. And they claim to experience the peace and comfort of God.

I happen to be among those people. And I personally know thousands of people—all good, smart, savvy, and wise individuals—who make that same claim. And I know of millions more.

What do you do with that claim?

Yes, you can find truly delusional people who claim the same things. But if a delusional person also believes that the earth orbits the sun, does that discredit the same belief among people who clearly aren't delusional? What about all the normal folks who have made and continue to make claims of experiencing God? How do we account for this? Is some "mass delusion" really the answer? Are proponents of atheism really the enlightened, intellectual few? Or do the claims of billions of people over thousands of years have a bit more weight than that? Let's put experiential evidence on the scale along with the other evidence we gave:

1. A caused universe.
2. A complex and sophisticated universe.
3. An innate moral law written on the hearts of every human being.
4. The claims of millions of rational, intelligent people.

I think that scale tips more toward believing that God exists than toward believing he does not.

But don't just trust my claims. Consider that since history began, some of humanity's greatest minds have examined the evidence and come to the same conclusion—minds that today we hold in highest honor for understanding and wisdom:

Moses—philosopher and political leader
Socrates—philosopher
Plato—philosopher
Aristotle—philosopher
Solomon—philosopher, poet, and king
The apostle Paul—philosopher and evangelist
Constantine the Great—emperor
Roger Bacon—philosopher, scientist, and originator of the Scientific Method
Hildegard of Bingen—theologian, writer, and first woman physician
Copernicus—priest, philosopher, and scientist
Galileo Galilei—scientist
Blaise Pascal—philosopher, mathematician, and scientist
Isaac Newton—scientist and mathematician
George Washington—general and president
Thomas Jefferson—philosopher and president
Benjamin Franklin—philosopher, scientist, and statesman
Michael Faraday—scientist
Abraham Lincoln—attorney and president
Harriet Tubman—civil rights champion
C. S. Lewis—professor, author, and theologian
J. R. R. Tolkien—professor and author
Helen Keller—author
Albert Einstein—scientist
James Irwin—astronaut
Mother Teresa—nun and humanitarian
Margaret Thatcher—stateswoman and prime minister
And many, many more.

They may not have all believed in the same God, or believed for the same reasons or to the same level, or shared the same religion. Yet nevertheless, unquestionably to an individual, they believed in the existence of a Creator. Why? Because the evidence was overwhelming. It still is.

God and the Soul

Let's look again at our evidence so far.

We know that we are destined to die.

We know that we have an eternal soul that lives on after we die.

We know that soul was created by an intelligent, eternal God.

We know that this same God gave us a moral code—a law—that he clearly expects us to live by.

We know that good and evil exist in the world, and that we are expected to be good.

So what does the sum of these things mean? What is God's purpose for the soul? At the end of this life amidst good and evil, what happens to the soul?

Is there a heaven?

Is there a hell?

And which will be our fate?

PART IV

Hell, No!
(You Don't Want to Go)

CHAPTER 13

What We Can't See Is Real

ONCE THERE WERE two friends who were avid baseball players. They had grown up playing Little League, then on their high school and college teams. Every summer as adults they continued to play in their local amateur leagues. Sadly, as they reached old age, they played less and less. But they both dreamed that just maybe heaven included baseball games. So they made a pact that whoever died first would let the other know whether baseball was played in heaven.

Finally, one of the friends did indeed pass on. After the funeral, the other friend went to the old ball park to reminisce about his buddy. As he sat there, he was stunned to see a ghostly image appear at home plate and come walking toward him. It was his friend, dressed in a heavenly baseball uniform. "I've got good news and bad news!" his ghostly pal cried out. "The good news is, there is baseball in heaven!"

"Oh, that's terrific!" replied the living buddy. "But what's the bad news?"

"You're pitching for the other team tomorrow night!"

That's the afterlife for you: good news and bad news. The good news is that there is an afterlife. The bad news is that there are two destinations in the afterlife. And one of them you're guaranteed not to like.

Can you guess that in this chapter we're going to talk about hell?

Now people don't like hell. Who would? (You could say that's sort of the point.) But if we just start off by not liking hell, we risk missing a very important truth that hell represents, and worse than that, we risk misunderstanding why there is a hell in the first place. So before we begin discussing the ins and outs of hell, we need to look at some core truths about the afterlife.

The first truth is that we need simply to understand how fundamentally important the afterlife is. We brought this idea up in the first chapter, when I asked you to confront the reality of your mortality. You are going to die. And you are going to spend a lot more time dead than you will ever spend alive. So to begin with, I want you to consider this thought: *The eternal is more significant than the temporary.* Scripture tells us, "For the things we see now will soon be gone, but the things we cannot see will last forever" (2 Cor. 4:18 NLT).

We tend to believe that the things we can see with our physical eyes are the only significant things out there. But according to Scripture a whole other life happens after we die, and it is far more significant than the life we live now. For one thing, the life we live now is so minuscule in the scheme of things that the whole of human history isn't so much as one-millionth of our universe's existence. But the life that comes later is eternal; it outdistances our universe by infinitely more than our universe outdistances us. Wouldn't you agree that the significance of eternity far outweighs the significance of a handful of decades?

As you weigh that truth, there are three eternal truths I want you to consider.

Eternal Truth #1: God Created Us to Love Us

One of the things we already determined was that our universe was made by an intelligent, purposeful designer: God. Well, that also means that you and I are each part of that intelligent, purposeful design. We have a reason to be here. We also have a reason behind why we, unlike all the rest of creation that we know of, are intelligent, spiritual beings, marvelously complex and wonderfully made. We are incredible works of the Creator's art. Furthermore, we are the only creatures that we know of capable of appreciating that very fact. Of all creation, we alone know that we are *created.*

So why did God create us? What in the world did he want people for? We are inferior to him in every way. We don't have anything he needs. We can't do anything he can't do for himself (and do better), and what we can do is pretty minuscule compared to the creative work he's already done. So why create us?

God created us to love us! Think of how much we love our children. We love our "creations," our children, so much that we are willing to do anything, even die, for them just to keep them safe and cared for. If we flawed and feeble humans have that instinct toward our own creations, how much more must God have those same feelings of love for and pride in us!

God created us to love us.

The Bible declares this very truth in no uncertain terms: " 'I have loved you with an everlasting love. And with unfailing love I have drawn you to myself' " (Jer. 31:3 NIV).

God's love lasts *forever.* You can't outlive God's love. You can't outrun God's love. You can't sin away God's love. It lasts past our mistakes. It lasts past our failures. It lasts past our shortcomings, our habits, and all of our hang-ups and screw-ups. You can't outgrow it and you can't oust it. God's love is permanent. God loves you no matter what.

Maybe you're reading this after having a bad week. Maybe you're reading this after committing multiple screw-ups. Maybe you have a track record of bad decisions and hateful choices. Maybe you've had bad news from a doctor, and suddenly death and God are staring you in the face and you're wondering what all that means. Well, the first reality of what all that means is that God loves you *no matter what.*

And here's the other thing about that fact: *God wants us to love him back.*

You know this. We all do. Why? Well, if I tell you I love my wife, don't you automatically expect that I want her to love me back? I love my children; don't I then want them to love me back? Oh, yes, I can love someone and have them not love me back. We see that all the time, and universally we know there's nothing sadder. We see the mother who desperately loves a daughter who has moved out and won't call. We see the boy who loves a father who pays him no attention. And we know that that mother and that little boy both want nothing more in the whole wide universe than to have their love returned. We make *movies* on that theme, whether the love is romantic or the love is between parent and child. Nothing causes us to pull out the tissues like a movie about unrequited love.

Why should God's love be any different? Love is about *relationship*, isn't it? We all know that love wants to be a two-way street—and God made us view love in that way. In fact, Jesus said the first and greatest commandment is that we love God with all our heart, soul, strength, and mind (Mark 12:30, paraphrased). God created us to love us and wants us to love him back.

Eternal Truth #2: God Designed Us for Eternity

We've already looked at this. We know that our bodies are not the true "us." The Bible says the body is a tent, a place you and I live in. If you've ever gone camping, by the way, you know that a tent is a temporary dwelling. A tent is not meant to be the place that you stay day in and day out. When you come to the end of a camping trip, you're done with the tent. You're ready to get back to your real, permanent home. When our lives end, we are done with our body tents. Our souls leave those tents for a permanent, eternal home. The tents of our bodies die, but as we have seen, the soul lives on, into eternity. God has built us to last forever.

The Bible says, "He [God] has also set eternity in the human heart" (Eccles. 3:11 NLT). There is an instinct, hardwired into every human being, that causes us to expect that our lives will go on forever, even amidst the certainty of death. The cross-cultural belief in some sort of life after death is evidence of this—we are designed to expect an afterlife. "God has set eternity in the human heart."

But let's look at it from a different angle. The word *heart* in Scripture often refers to "the inner man," or the soul, and that's the context being used in this passage. If that's so, then you can see that God has indeed built us to last forever, because he has put eternity into "the inner man": eternity is a built-in characteristic of the soul. Our "inner man" will never die; it will be alive, somehow and somewhere.

Eternal Truth #3: God Divided Eternity into Two Places

Yes, that's right. I said "two." Not one, but two. Not three, either. Just two. The Bible calls these two places heaven and hell.

Jesus says, "In My Father's house are many rooms" (John 14:2). We'll deal with that in the next chapter, but for now, let's just say that (metaphorically speaking) God has a big, big house with lots and lots of rooms. Jesus continues, "If it were not so, I would have told you. I am going to prepare a place for you. And if I go to prepare a place for you, I will come back and take you to be with me, that you may also be where I am" (John 14:2–3 NIV). Obviously, Jesus is talking about heaven—his Father's house.

But notice how Jesus describes heaven. He describes it as a *place.* Atheism likes to claim that people "make up" heaven in order to feel better about death or whatever bad things happen to them on earth. But Jesus himself pretty much pooh-poohs that argument. He specifically says it's a place and "If it were not so, I would have told you." In other words, Jesus is saying, "Don't believe anyone who argues I'm just trying to make you feel better or that you're just imagining something. I am saying that heaven is real."

But atheism does have one thing right: it's easy to believe in heaven. We don't have any problem with that. A wonderful, eternal resort where there is no pain or suffering or poverty or wickedness, and everyone we've ever loved surrounds us, and everything is beautiful and perfect? Yeah, sign us up! According to a survey of Americans, over 75 percent of us believe in heaven, and over 80 percent believe in an afterlife in general. Of those Americans who believe in heaven, nearly 100 percent believe they will wind up there.[1] They believe this because their measuring stick is whether their "good" behavior outweighs their "bad" behavior. By that measuring stick, it's easy to conclude that the answer is yes. Most people look at themselves and say, "Well, I really haven't done anything that bad. I haven't murdered anybody lately, I haven't broken into anybody's house. I'm good. So I'm going to heaven." Our problem is not with heaven. Our problem is with hell.

The Bad News We Don't Want to Hear

You see, that same survey also revealed that while 71 percent of us also believe in hell, only a third believe it is an actual place and less than half of 1 percent believe that they personally are headed there.[2] Of course, this result is not particularly surprising. After all, who wants to believe the bad things in the Bible? We've got enough bad things to deal with in life. Let's just rip out the bad stuff and discard it. Heaven's good. Everybody loves heaven. Nobody loves hell.

When I was in my early twenties, I went into New York City to attend a Christian concert. We took the subway, and when we got to the entrance, a preacher was there. This guy was literally on top of a soapbox, with his Bible in his hand, screaming, "You're going to be judged! You're going to burn in hell! You sinners are going to hell! You smokers are going to hell! You alcoholics are going to hell! You homosexuals are going to hell!" And he went on and on and on about every single sin he could think of.

Now, obviously, this guy thought that screaming about hell at people was what God wanted him to do. Yet nobody would stop to listen to this guy. And I thought, *Here am I, a believer in Christ. I ought to punch that guy in the face as hard as I can and knock him off that soapbox. Because the message that he's preaching is not the gospel message.*

In my opinion the gospel message is summed up in 2 Corinthians 5:19: "God was reconciling the world to himself in Christ, not counting people's sins against them. And he has committed to us the message of reconciliation." That's been my guiding principal from the beginning of my Christian life. I'm not a hellfire-and-brimstone preacher. I don't like the topic of hell any more than you do. So I don't believe God wants me to preach hell or condemn people or even scare people into heaven.

But I'm not going to tell you that hell doesn't exist, or that it's a fancy metaphor for the bad things in life, just so you'll feel better about me or religion. As much as I hate the idea of it, I am convinced that hell exists—that it is in fact a very real and eternal place. We'll look more closely at that next.

CHAPTER 14

Visions of Hell

REMEMBER THE NEAR-DEATH experiences from chapter 5? One thing we noted about these NDEs was that they all seemed to be positive. Hell didn't seem to be a factor. So you might be inclined to think that hell really isn't an element of the afterlife. But indeed, negative NDEs *have* been recorded. There are in fact people who have died and experienced hell.

Maurice Rawlings was a doctor with an incredible professional pedigree. The former personal physician to President Dwight D. Eisenhower and the Joint Chiefs of Staff, he was one of the leading cardiologists in the United States and an expert in the field of medical life support. As a cardiologist, Dr. Rawlings was often in place to revive patients during cardiac arrest. For him it had become just part of the job. But one day that job took a decidedly spiritual turn.

While doing treadmill tests under Dr. Rawlings's supervision, a patient collapsed. The test monitors showed that the man's heart had stopped. He was dead. Dr. Rawlings immediately began CPR. Suddenly, the man revived and screamed, "I am in hell!" He then died a second time. Dr. Rawlings continued working to revive him, and the patient came back again. "Don't stop!" the man cried out. The patient's pupils were heavily dilated, and the man was trembling in apparent terror. "Don't you understand?" the man pleaded. "I am in hell. Each time you quit I go back to hell! Don't let me go back to hell!"

Dr. Rawlings was focused on installing an emergency pacemaker. The patient again died—no heartbeat, no breathing. Again Dr. Rawlings revived him, a process that continued several more times, with the patient becoming increasingly panicked with each revival. Finally, the patient gasped, "How do I stay out of hell?"

Dr. Rawlings happened to be a Christian and told the man to ask Jesus to help. "I don't know how," replied the terrified patient. "Pray for me!"

Dr. Rawlings led the man in a prayer, made up on the spot: "Lord Jesus, I ask you to keep me out of hell. Forgive my sins. I turn my life over to you. If I die, I want to go to heaven. If I live, I'll be [in your service] forever."

After the prayer, the patient died and was revived again, but his hell complaints ceased. Dr. Rawlings managed to stabilize the man and transported him into hospital care.

A few days later, Dr. Rawlings interviewed his patient and asked if the man had any further experience with hell. "What hell?" asked the patient. "I don't recall any hell!" The man didn't remember anything bad that had happened—none of the terror or pleading. But he did remember praying to Jesus and firmly clung to his newfound faith. He even shared that after the prayer, he had traveled out of his body, watched the doctor work, and then met several deceased relatives, including his mother (who had died when he was an infant) and stepmother. He also described an experience with a brilliant beam of light in a lush valley filled with beautiful colors. Despite the unusual circumstances behind the prayer, and his failure to remember the cause, the man remained a devout Christian for the rest of his life.[1]

Other sources provide accounts similar to those recorded by Dr. Rawlings, including accounts by people who became Christians or even ministers as a result of their experiences. Among these are the Reverend Howard Storm, formerly an art professor and adamant atheist; Dr. Kenneth Hagin, who at the time of his vision was only a "cultural" Christian; Dr. George Ritchie, a young soldier at the time of his near-death experience; Ronald Reagan (not the president), a nonbeliever who died from injuries in a street fight; and Matthew Botsford, a businessman and agnostic who died, was revived, and went into a coma after falling victim to a random shooting. Although such accounts can vary widely, certain few key elements are often present:

- a descent into the ground or an impression of being in a vast underground cavern
- a region of great heat or possibly fire
- dim, reddish light
- a malevolent presence or malevolent beings
- humans engaged in acts of brutality or depravity toward one another
- a pervasive feeling of self-loathing and despair, and a total absence of hope or love
- a loving presence that pulls them out and returns them to life, or to a positive NDE; this usually happens after a specific request for help made by the individual, often addressed to Christ

Not all accounts share these elements, though the aura of despair and hopelessness seems to be universal, and all shared a conviction that hell was indeed real and they never wished to experience it again. Matthew Botsford echoed the sentiments of many, saying, "I want people to know that hell is real and it's a place that definitely has to be avoided."[2]

To me that last idea is the whole point.

Hell is a real place, and you don't want to go there.

CHAPTER 15

So Why Is Hell Hard to Believe?

ONE OF THE main reasons I believe hell exists is because I also believe that the devil exists. And by the devil I don't mean some guy with horns, a pointy tail, and a pitchfork. I mean an active, intelligent being who wants to separate us from God. My biblical belief in the devil is based on the evidence of all the odd twists and hoops people will go through *not* to believe in God—and all the efforts people make to try to keep others from believing in God. One of those efforts is to insist that there is no hell.

You see, if the devil can get us to believe there is no hell, what do we need a Savior for? If there are no consequences for our sins, what do we need this guy called Jesus Christ for? If there is no hell, what urgency will a guy like me, a follower of Christ, have to share the message of Christ? Why would I bother to write this book? Why would I tell you about the importance of dealing with death if there is no hell and everybody just goes to heaven? Why would you even need to know?

In the 1800s, a notorious criminal named Charles Peace was convicted of murder and sentenced to be hanged. While awaiting his execution, Peace heard a chaplain reading aloud about hell and was amazed that the chaplain read the passage with so little emotion. Peace admonished the chaplain, saying, "Sir, if I believed what you say that you believe, even if England were covered with broken glass from coast to coast, I would walk over it, if need be, on hands and knees and think it worthwhile living, just to save one soul from an eternal hell like that!"[1]

If a murderer can admit to how a belief in hell would have motivated him to warn others about it, we can understand why God's greatest enemy (and ours) wouldn't want anyone to believe in hell. Out of sight, out of mind.

Justice or Torture?

Another reason people don't believe in hell is because they don't believe it reflects real justice, particularly if the Christian point of view is true. A nonbeliever will say, "You mean that if I don't profess Jesus Christ as my Lord and Savior, but I live a morally good life and help others, my fate is to spend eternity in hell, in punishment and torment—just because I didn't believe what you believe? What kind of justice is that?"

A prominent atheist named Charles Templeton argued, "I couldn't hold someone's hand to a fire for a moment. Not an instant! How can a loving God, just because you don't obey him and do what he wants, torture you forever—not allowing you to die, but to continue in that pain for eternity?"[2]

Nobody likes hell. And since we don't like it, don't think it's just, we don't believe in hell.

The problem with the arguments I've just mentioned is the people involved are not talking about the real hell. They have a picture of hell, but that picture does not come from the Bible or the teachings of Christ. It comes instead from the fourteenth-century epic Italian poem *Inferno* by Dante Alighieri. *Inferno* gives a guided tour of hell, in which the narrator witnesses all the torments of the damned souls. It's an imaginative masterpiece of literature, depicting a hell of raging fires (and, paradoxically, frozen lakes), demonic jailers, and nine descending layers of ever more gruesome torture. But Dante's poem is not a religious work at all. It's political satire, aimed at Dante's political and personal enemies, as well as a call for earthly political reform. The tortures Dante describes reflect his opinions of the crimes he believed his opponents had committed. Yet it is Dante's depiction of hell that has become the standard image in Western thought ever since: a horrid prison of endless torment, populated by leering demons—the home of the devil himself. Another poet, the English Puritan John Milton, echoed that same theme in the epic poem *Paradise Lost,* when he had the devil build a city and palace in hell.

But is that really hell? It's certainly not the home of the devil, but is it a physical torture chamber?

CHAPTER 16

Why Hell?

I KNOW YOU MAY not believe in Christianity. You aren't ready to just take the Bible's word, Jesus' word, or mine for the existence of hell. Will you accept the teachings of your heart?

Do you love justice? Remember how in a previous chapter we discussed the evidence of the innate moral law? All of us, we acknowledged, have innate expectations of the way people should behave toward one another. But even more than that, we have an innate sense of justice. We write novels and plays and television shows and movies about justice. We build whole societies out of a desire to create and defend justice. We launch wars because we desire justice. Just as we have eternity wired into our hearts, we have the desire for justice wired in as well.

So when do we get it?

We don't get justice on earth. We all know that. The nineteen hijackers who flew the planes into the Twin Towers, the Pentagon, and the soil of Pennsylvania can never be brought to earthly justice for the thousands of lives they took. Osama bin Laden, who ordered those same attacks, may have been killed, but does that fate alone seem like justice? Adolf Hitler died in his bunker, but was that justice for the brutality of the concentration camps and the deaths of six million Jews, or the millions of other deaths from the war he started? And what about Joseph Stalin or Chairman Mao, who together slaughtered millions more people than even Hitler, yet who both died peacefully and still in power. What justice did they receive? None on this earth.

Yet God has wired us not only to demand justice, but also to *expect it.* If we didn't expect justice, we would not be disappointed when we fail to see it. Animals don't expect justice. Plants don't expect justice. Only people do. We'll even go so far as to demand justice on the *behalf* of animals, and yes, even plants, through laws against cruelty to animals or harming the environment. Why do we have this expectation? We have it because God put this expectation in us. Which means that God also desires and expects justice, as much as or more than we do.

Thomas Jefferson once said, referring to slavery, "Indeed I tremble for my country when I reflect that God is just, that his justice cannot sleep forever."[1] Jefferson knew that for justice, by definition, to exist, God himself must be just. And if God himself must be just, then God *will* act to bring about justice.

So, again, when do we get that justice? If it doesn't happen on earth in this life, the only answer as to when God will bring about justice must be in the afterlife. And that, perhaps, should make us all tremble. I may want and expect justice on my behalf for the things done to me and to others, but I'm less than eager to desire justice over the things I have done.

In short, justice doesn't reject hell. Justice demands it.

For Whom Was Hell Made?

I can't really define hell to you. I've never been there, never seen it, and don't want to, either. So I'm going to defer to someone who knew what he was talking about when it came to the facts about hell. And that someone was Jesus.

Unlike the "nice" Jesus some people prefer today, who wouldn't ruffle feathers or threaten anybody, the Jesus in the Bible was never reluctant to express his opinions or invoke strong justice. He had no problem discussing hell, and he clearly believed it existed. Jesus went so far as to directly threaten certain people with hell! But it's interesting to note who Jesus' main targets for that threat actually were: religious people. Uh-oh. When Jesus spoke about hell, he was usually talking to or about the religious leaders of his day. He would call them "sons of hell" (Matt. 23:15 NKJV) or "children of [their] father, the devil" (John 8:44 NLT). He would say that whoever went so far as to call another person a "fool" (by implication, to curse them) was in danger of "hell fire" (Matt. 5:22 NKJV). He didn't reserve hell for just murderers or burglars; he included calling someone an idiot as a damning offense before God. Uh-oh.

But were these statements threats or warnings? Let's look at the reality of what Jesus taught about hell.

In a key passage Jesus was addressing the phony behavior of religious people who talked a lot about God, but ignored their fellow men. The passage ends this way: "Then he will say to those on his left, 'Depart from me, you who are cursed, into the eternal fire prepared for the devil and his angels'" (Matt. 25:41 NIV).

I don't want you to get the wrong idea about God. If somebody tells you that Christianity teaches that God made hell in order to punish people, that person is wrong. Christianity teaches nothing of the sort. God never prepared hell for people. We are the love of his life. He *never* had us in mind when he thought about hell. This verse, Matthew 25:41, even says as much: God prepared hell *for the devil.* And I don't mean God made hell to be the devil's anti-heaven. Dante and Milton and Hollywood are wrong. Hell is not the devil's playground or the devil's home base. The devil is not in hell and has never been there. That's pure fiction, and the Bible doesn't teach that at all.

Jesus is saying that hell was made as the final, eternal prison for the devil. Revelation says that when this world comes to an end, the devil will be cast into the lake of fire (Rev. 20:10). So clearly hell is the last place the devil wants to be. It was made for him, to be the final fate of evil, imprisoned once and for all, forever. That's why hell was made.

So Why Are People There?

To answer that question, let's consider a parable Jesus tells about hell. It starts this way: "There was a certain rich man who was clothed in purple and fine linen and fared sumptuously every day" (Luke 16:19 NKJV).

This guy was not just your assembly-line rich guy. In the original language, this guy was superrich. Every day he ate incredibly expensive meals—this guy wasn't ordering off the dollar menu at the local Burger King. He wore the best clothes, too. In those days anyone who could afford to wear dyed cloth was rich, but anyone who wore cloth dyed in purple was rich beyond measure. Purple was the color of royalty; Caesar himself wore purple because only kings and emperors could afford it. As for "fine linen," that was the cloth of cloth. This guy wasn't wearing blue jeans and polyester; he had tailored Armani suits that would have made James Bond jealous. He wasn't just ordinary "I think I'll buy an island" rich; he was "I think I'll buy Rhode Island" rich.

Jesus is telling this story to a bunch of people who have no idea where he's going with it. But he has their attention, because we all love to hear about rich people. You remember the TV series *MTV Cribs*, which showed us people with mansions and luxury cars and yachts. The producers of that show got rich just by telling people how rich other people were—that's how much we like to hear about rich people. And Jesus knew this.

Then Jesus says, "But there was a certain beggar named Lazarus, full of sores, who was laid at his gate, desiring to be fed with the crumbs which fell from the rich man's table. Moreover the dogs came and licked his sores" (Luke 16:20–21 NKJV).

Well, that's quite a change. We go from this superrich guy to this dirt-poor guy. Actually, Lazarus was poorer than that. He was so poor he couldn't even afford a couple of Band-Aids for his sores. He just let the dogs come up and lick them clean.

Notice also the phrase about Lazarus wanting to eat the crumbs from the rich man's table. In Bible days, they didn't have forks. People just picked up their food with their hands. They hadn't even invented the sandwich yet. So people's hands tended to get rather messy. Now an ordinary person might just wipe his hands on his outfit. But when you're wearing purple linen, you don't do that. Even the superrich don't want to muss a tailored suit. Instead, the rich used bits of bread to wipe off their hands, letting the filthy scraps fall on the table. The servants would collect these dirty bread scraps and fling them outside for whatever or whoever might eat them. So now you know why Lazarus was outside the man's house, and why the dogs were hanging around with Lazarus. They weren't his pets; they just wanted to snap up the scraps thrown outside the gate.

Jesus has set up the ultimate contrast. On the one hand, we've got a guy so rich he can buy the world. On the other hand, we've got a guy so poor he's fighting dogs for scraps. By now Jesus' listeners are locked in. Then Jesus hits them with his first point—and he does it by killing off his two main characters.

"So it was that the beggar died, and was carried by the angels to Abraham's bosom. The rich man also died and was buried. And being in torments in Hades, he lifted up his eyes and saw Abraham afar off, and Lazarus in his bosom" (Luke 16:22–23 NKJV).

Now we've seen this point before. Death does not discriminate. Everyone, whether filthy rich or dirt poor, is going to die. Death is the great equalizer.

But Jesus' story, and his point, doesn't end there, because Jesus wants his listeners to think about death but, more important, to think about what happens after. Now Jesus knows he can't just talk about death and get everybody to tune in. So he leads his listeners to the topic with these two characters.

> Then he [the rich man] cried and said, "Father Abraham, have mercy on me, and send Lazarus that he may dip the tip of his finger in water and cool my tongue; for I am tormented in this flame." But Abraham said, "Son, remember that in your lifetime you received your good things, and likewise

> Lazarus evil things; but now he is comforted and you are tormented. And besides all this, between us and you there is a great gulf fixed, so that those who want to pass from here to you cannot, nor can those from there pass to us."
>
> Then he said, "I beg you therefore, father, that you would send him to my father's house, for I have five brothers, that he may testify to them, lest they also come to this place of torment." Abraham said to him, "They have Moses and the prophets; let them hear them." And he said, "No, father Abraham; but if one goes to them from the dead, they will repent." But he said to him, "If they do not hear Moses and the prophets, neither will they be persuaded though one rise from the dead." (Luke 16:24–31 NKJV)

Jesus is making several points in this parable, but in the details he's also teaching us some interesting things about death. The first is this: *After we die, we keep on living.* Or, to put it another way, God created us to live forever.

Notice that the rich man and the poor man both died, but they both kept on living. Their bodies may have given out, but their souls stayed alive.

The second point Jesus makes is this: *After death, you go to one of two eternal places.*

Not just one eternal place. Not three or more. Two. You go to one or you go to the other. You don't get to sit it all out.

And Jesus makes it quite plain that these two places are heaven and hell. The rich guy goes to the hell side, the poor guy goes to the heaven side. There is no in-between place. There is no place you can go if you weren't really good or really bad and earn your place into heaven in some sort of afterlife merit system. After all, Scripture is clear: we are saved by grace through faith, "not of works, lest any man should boast" (Eph. 2:9 KJV). There's no half-way house for good behavior mentioned anywhere in the Bible. No, it's heaven or hell.

In chapter 2, we read another parable about a rich man who

died. You may remember that we excluded wealth as the cause of his death. The same thing applies to hell. Riches don't cause you to die, and they don't send you to hell (otherwise Abraham would have been with the rich guy, not Lazarus). So the rich man isn't in hell because of his wealth. He is in hell because he loved his riches but did not love his fellow man. He ignored God and God's commandments. He didn't listen to the message of the prophets. He didn't think about eternal things until it was too late. And hell was his fate.

The third point that Jesus makes is this: *Once you are dead, there are no second chances.* Look at what Abraham says to the rich man: "And besides all this, between us and you there is a great gulf fixed." In other words, Jesus is saying that once you die, where you end up is permanent.

Of course, we don't like that. It makes us uncomfortable. We would much rather it be that you live life any old way you want to, forget about God, die, take a look behind door number 1 and see hell, and then choose door number 2. But that's not really a choice for God, nor is it a choice we get to make after death. Our choice must be made now, when it can be an act of love, not later, when it would be nothing but another act of selfishness at the end of a self-centered life.

So once we die, our eternal destination is fixed. There are no second chances. We need to decide here and now, in this life, whether or not we will love God. That's the deal.

CHAPTER 17

Three Bad Words

SIGNIFICANTLY, JESUS TALKED about hell several other times in the New Testament. It's important to note that our word *hell* is not one Jesus ever used. It's a word descended from the ancient Norse word *Hel*. In Norse myth, Hel was the land of the dead, which was divided into nine levels, the lowest of which was a place of eternal torment for the wicked. Sound familiar?

Once you use a word to represent something from another language, you wind up with all the connotations and assumptions that word carries with it. On the DVD set of the classic British comedy *Monty Python and the Holy Grail*, there's a version of the movie dubbed in Japanese that was then translated back into English subtitles. The result is unrecognizable compared to the original English script. All the English meanings and connotations have been lost; the Japanese didn't get the English jokes, and English speakers didn't get the Japanese replacements.

With the word *hell* it gets even more complicated, because not only does it have the connotations of its original pagan origins, but, as we saw in chapter 15, it has the ideas and imagery of medieval artists and poets, nineteenth-century evangelists, modern artists and poets, and even Hollywood all bundled together. We've got everything from Dante and Milton to horror movies like *Drag Me to Hell*.

So if we're going to discuss the real hell, we need to drop all that baggage and start with a blank slate. We can then draw onto that slate only what the Bible has to say about hell.

How Does Jesus Describe Hell?

The Gospels have Jesus using two words that are often translated as "hell" and also have Jesus offering descriptive phrases without giving the place a specific name. The entire New Testament includes three names for hell, two used by Jesus and the third used by the apostle Peter and referenced by Jude. These three names are Gehenna, Hades, and Tartaros (in Latin and English, Tartarus).

(Note that we know Jesus spoke Aramaic, not Greek, so even the Greek names are a translation of whatever names he actually used!)

In Matthew 5:22, 29, and 30, Jesus refers to "the fires of Gehenna" and being "thrown into Gehenna." "Gehenna" was an Aramaic name for the Valley of Hinnom, which lay just outside the city of Jerusalem. During the days of the kingdom of Judah, this valley was used by apostate kings for human sacrifices to the pagan god Molech. Part of these sacrifices involved "passing" children "through the fire" (see 2 Chron. 33:6; 2 Kings 23:10; Jer. 33:35). Small wonder that the place became associated with evil and fiery torment. The good King Josiah destroyed these altars, but the valley was considered cursed. Isaiah referred to it as the final site where the corpses of God's enemies would be dumped to rot and burn (Isa. 66:24). Some late Jewish traditions claim that the city garbage was collected into this valley and burned, and there is evidence that the Roman legions stationed in Jerusalem used the area for cremation (a practice abhorrent to devout Jews). It is possible that these cremations included executed criminals—nobody much cared to waste time burying dead murderers. So to the Jews of Jesus' day, Gehenna had come to mean a cursed place of death, destruction, constant fire, and burning corpses, as well as the final destination of criminals. As a metaphor for hell, it was an obvious choice. So when Jesus used the name Gehenna for hell, he was following a tradition already practiced by everyone in the region.

The second name, Hades, is from Greek and Roman mythology, in those days the religion common to everybody who wasn't a Jew. Hades was the land of the dead, and the pagans believed it was divided into three different regions. One region was the land of the blessed, or the Elysian Fields, where good people and great heroes went (equivalent in some ways to heaven, although the gods did not live in this paradise, aside from the god of death, his servants, and his part-time wife—none of whom really wanted to live there). Another region was generally referred to as Hades itself, a place where the ordinary dead, who had been neither particularly good nor particularly evil, were gathered. It was neither pleasant nor unpleasant; the sort of place where you just said, "Well, here I am. I guess I'm dead." So in at least one sense, Hades was a catchall name for the land of the dead; in another sense it might include a sort of hell, as we saw in the rich man/Lazarus parable: "The rich man also died and was buried. And being in torments in Hades, he lifted up his eyes and saw Abraham afar off, and Lazarus in his bosom" (Luke 16:22–23 NKJV).

Last is Tartaros, the place where the most outrageously evil people went and suffered endless, pointless toil or other torments as punishment for their crimes. *Tartaros* is literally translated as "the deep place," referring to its location in Hades. Tartaros is used in 2 Peter 2:4 to refer to the place of imprisonment for the fallen angels awaiting final judgment. Peter's usage is actually the verb form, "to throw into the deep place [or Tartaros]," rather than an actual place name, and may be an allusion to the Greek myth about the Titans, powerful beings overthrown by the gods and imprisoned in Tartarus, a story his Greek audience would have known well. Jude makes a reference to imprisoned angels that echoes Peter's statement (Jude 1:6), though he does not give the place a name.

So when Jesus talks about hell, he is using one of the first two names. He knew the connotations of those names for his listeners and would naturally expect them to imagine the cultural pictures they had of what those names meant. But did he mean those pictures to be taken literally?

Let's look at what Jesus had to say about hell.

Hell Is a Place Full of Fire

Most people today picture hell as a physical torture chamber where people are burned forever. And indeed, Jesus' description of the rich man's experience in hell seems to indicate flames: "And being in torments in Hades, [the rich man] . . . cried and said, 'Father Abraham, have mercy on me, and send Lazarus that he may dip the tip of his finger in water and cool my tongue; for I am tormented in this flame'" (Luke 16:23–24 NKJV[NM).

In other places, Jesus describes hell as having everlasting heat: "If your hand causes you to stumble, cut it off. It is better for you to enter life maimed than with two hands to go into hell, where the fire never goes out" (Mark 9:43 NIV).

Revelation chapters 20–21 refer to a "lake of everlasting fire" into which the devil, the beast (or the anti-Christ), the false prophet, and "the cowardly, the unbelieving, the vile, the murderers, the sexually immoral, those who practice magic arts, the idolaters and all liars" all get tossed (Rev. 21:8 NIV). (This reference, by the way, is what our culture has come to name "hell," though Revelation gives it no specific name at all.)

So whatever you call it, the Bible seems to say in no uncertain terms that in hell there are flames.

Hell Is Full of Darkness

But the Bible also says that in hell there is darkness: "The subjects of the kingdom will be thrown outside, into the darkness, where there will be weeping and gnashing of teeth" (Matt. 8:12 NIV); "God did not spare angels when they sinned, but sent them to hell, putting them in chains of darkness to be held for judgment" (2 Pet. 2:4 NIV).

But wait. How can you have both utter darkness and intense

flames in the same place? If I sit in my den at midnight with all the lights off, it can be a very dark room. But if I then make a roaring fire in my fireplace, the room is no longer dark. And the more intense the fire is, the brighter the light is. Everybody knows that the sun is basically a huge ball of fire, hot beyond imagining. And it is also the source of light for our entire world. So how can you have intense flames and utter darkness? The answer is, *you can't.*

Contradiction or Imagery?

So what's going on? Is Jesus contradicting himself? Does he not know what he is talking about?

Not at all. If you study the life of Jesus, you will see that he constantly used strong, descriptive imagery to make his points. That was the style of teachers of the day, and we even mimic it today in fields as far ranging as the ministry and science. In my own ministry I will use illustrations, personal stories, and even popular culture to explain my ideas. Physicists use words like *clockwise* and *strings* and *spin* to describe things that are neither clocks nor strings or spinning. Does that mean we are contradicting ourselves or don't know what we're talking about? No. It means we're using words that our listeners do understand to help them imagine complex ideas that can't be truly defined.

Jesus, for example, loved to speak in parables. The story we've just been looking at, about the rich man and Lazarus, is a parable. That means it's a piece of fiction, made up by the speaker to illustrate a point. When Jesus told the parable of the prodigal son, he wasn't talking about an actual person. When Jesus told the parable of the lost sheep, he wasn't talking about an actual sheep or an actual shepherd. He was making up a story that his listeners could relate to, to teach them something about God. The individual elements of the story aren't meant to be taken literally; they're meant to be taken figuratively. They *represent* a truth about spiritual things, not the actual nature of those things.

In the parable of the rich man and Lazarus, Jesus is teaching his listeners and us truths about the afterlife by using the symbolic imagery of the day. He acknowledges that there is a heaven, there is a hell, and our choices in life affect our fate in eternity. But Jesus is not actually teaching the physical nature of either heaven or hell. He is simply working within the framework of what his listeners already assumed to get at the truth behind it all. The parable exists to correct his listeners' assumptions about the nature of who was blessed and who was not, what it is God actually values in our lives, and how our choices about God affect our final fate. It does not exist to be a literal description of the afterlife, like some sort of first-century *Frommer's Guide to Heaven and Hell.*

So what does this parable tell us about hell? Well, throughout the scriptures, flames are often used as a symbol for judgment. Jesus' listeners knew this and expected it. When Jesus described the place where the rich man went after death, he was merely echoing the image of that place his listeners already had: a place with the burning fires of judgment. Jesus was illustrating a point; he was not necessarily trying to describe an actual physical torture chamber. The flames were there because the people of that culture expected them. Jesus' point was that hell is a place where nobody wants to be. If for his listeners that meant flames, then flames were what he described. If it meant darkness, then darkness was what he described.

Think again about the descriptions Jesus used. He compared hell to the cursed Valley of Hinnom with its perpetual flames (Matt. 5:22, 29–30). Now the fires there may have been constant, but what about the stuff tossed into them? Did yesterday's spoiled rags just keep burning forever in the dump? Of course not.

As British pastor and theologian John R. W. Stott points out, "The fire [of hell] is termed 'eternal' and 'unquenchable,' but it would be very odd if what is thrown into it proves indestructible. Our expectation would be the opposite: it would be consumed forever, not tormented forever."[1]

Look again at Jesus' words about Gehenna: "If your hand

causes you to stumble, cut it off. It is better for you to enter life maimed than with two hands to go into hell [Gehenna], where the fire never goes out" (Mark 9:43 NIV). When Jesus says the bit about cutting off one's hand, we know he's not talking about literal self-mutilation. Why, then, do we assume he's talking about literal flames that never stop burning whatever is put in them? Both notions are preposterous, and clearly aren't what Jesus meant. He was saying to people, "Look, if they were going to toss you into the rubbish fire for something you did, wouldn't you much prefer they just toss in the hand that did it rather than your whole body? It's the same way with hell. You're far better off getting rid of whatever selfish attitudes and beliefs are causing you to act against God, no matter how emotionally painful that would be, than spending eternity suffering the consequences for clinging to those things."

So Jesus described his ideas in terms that the people of his day could understand, and hell was no exception. For example, when Jesus described hell as a place "where the worm does not die and the fire is not quenched," he is actually quoting Isaiah 66:24—and that quote itself was a metaphorical reference to the Valley of Hinnom. Once again, Jesus was referring to the cursed valley with its burning rubbish and corpses, along with the maggots and other vermin one would expect to find there. In other words, a very ugly place.

So in his own words about hell, Jesus is creating a metaphor with a powerful message: *hell is a horrible place.* According to further scripture, like Revelation 21, which pictures the final judgment of the devil and those who reject God as being cast into the lake of fire, hell is only going to get even more horrible. That's Jesus' point. That's his intended message. It's not about the flames or the worms or the darkness. It's about the utter horror of hell, one that exceeds even our wildest imaginations. Jesus is saying, "What's the worst place you can think of? Well, that's what hell is like. So make sure you don't go there."

CHAPTER 18

Hell Without the Drama

If Jesus was using metaphor in the places where he talked about hell, is there ever a moment when he didn't use metaphor, when he revealed what the real hell is like? Yes, there is. It happened in the Garden of Gethsemane.

I want you to picture the scene. It's night. There are no lights except the stars in the sky and the glimmer of flames from a campfire where the disciples have gathered, wondering what has their teacher so upset. Jesus moves off into the garden by himself, to be alone with God—his Father, in every sense of the word. There he thinks about the day ahead. He knows what's coming. He knows he'll soon be arrested and tried unlawfully, convicted, whipped, beaten, and crucified. And he knows he's going to die. In this moment he is so tormented, so in anguish that he sweats drops of blood as he cries out to his Father.

Why?

Yes, the whipping and the beating and the death will be excruciatingly painful, and Jesus knows it. You and I wouldn't be too happy about that. But unlike you and me, Jesus knows that's all temporary. He knows that God will raise him from the dead. He knows that he will eventually return to his Father's side and reign as Lord over all creation. If you were told you had to endure momentary excruciating pain, but once it was over you would be completely healed, pain-free, and have everything you ever dreamed of, wouldn't you do it? Yes, you'd be worried about the pain, but would you be in anguish over it? I think not. So what is Jesus in anguish over?

What had Jesus struggling can be summed up in the question he would eventually cry from the cross: "My God, my God—why have you forsaken me?"

For Jesus, the worst possible fate imaginable was to be absent from God. Going to a place where God was absent was the fate Jesus feared, even though that fate was temporary. He didn't sweat blood because he was worried about physical torture. He sweated blood because he knew he was going to be separated from the Father, a state of being he had never known. It is that anguish more than anything else that I believe Jesus was trying to communicate in all his metaphors for hell.

So Why Talk About Flames and Darkness?

Unlike Christ, you and I are already separated from God. It isn't a final, permanent severing, but at the same time we don't have any knowledge of the depth of love that God's full presence really is. Jesus did, but how does one communicate that to people who don't have any comprehension of it? How do you describe an ocean to a desert nomad, or a desert to a Polynesian islander? All you can do is choose the closest possible metaphors and hope they get your point.

If you tell a modern atheist that hell is a place of eternal separation from God, you may hear, "So what?" As far as the atheist is concerned, that's no different from his current state. And there are people who've been given such a mixed-up view of God (mostly due to mixed-up, legalistic Christians) that they may even welcome the idea. "No God pointing his finger at me and telling me I'm a sinner? Sign me up!" It's not the worst fate they can imagine because they really don't understand what it means.

Here on earth, we are surrounded by the blessings of God.

God, after all, is the Creator—everything we think of as good exists because he makes it exist. Sunlight, wind, and rain, cool water and fresh fruit, the beauty of nature and the majesty of night: all are the blessings of God, showered "on the just and on the unjust" (Matt. 5:45 KJV). We experience these on earth whether we want them or not and whether we believe in God or not. Likewise we know that kindness, mercy, justice, freedom, compassion, friendship, laughter, and love are all the creations of God. He conceived of all good things. They come from him and from no other source.

But if God were to leave the earth, to truly give us ultimate separation from him, all goodness would necessarily depart with him. God could no more leave goodness behind in a place he didn't exist in than you or I could leave our brains behind to watch a football game while our bodies slipped into the kitchen for a quick snack. Goodness is inherent to God, and God is inherent to goodness. When we say that hell is eternal separation from God, we mean that hell is eternal separation from God *and everything he produces and is*: Light. Beauty. Mercy. Justice. Compassion. Love. If God is gone, these things are gone. That is the true horror of hell, and it's a situation we find almost impossible to comprehend.

So is Jesus being misleading about hell when he describes flames and darkness?

No more than you would be misleading using whatever words you could come up with to describe that ocean to the desert nomad. Let's say you told him, "The ocean is like the desert, only the dunes are made of water, not sand." You've achieved a very picturesque image that does convey the idea of waves, but in reality the waves in the ocean are nothing like dunes at all. You're not lying—you've just chosen something he understands to represent something he doesn't. In the same way, Jesus chose the metaphors and ideas about hell that his listeners understood to convey the concept of a place they would not want to be.

But Jesus did explain what hell was really like: "The subjects of the kingdom will be thrown outside, into the darkness, where there will be weeping and gnashing of teeth" (Matt. 8:12 NIV).

What does Jesus mean by "gnashing of teeth"? Does he mean people are chewing something? Not at all. "Gnashing of teeth" was an expression of the day describing a moment when someone realized they had suffered an incredible loss, often as the result of an irreparable mistake. When Jesus uses this phrase, he is describing that very situation. He doesn't mean that everyone is grinding their teeth all the time in some sort of dental nightmare. He means that the people in hell are forced to realize they have lost something of great and eternal value, which they can never regain. The regret, anger, and rage in hell don't occur because it has flames or darkness, but because those in hell realize that the God they thumbed their noses at their whole lives was really God. Those in hell realize that the Savior they rejected as Christ really was who he said he was. They realize that there was more to life than just the lives they lived here on earth; that there really was a hell to shun and a heaven to gain.

That's a pain much greater than any type of physical torture one would have to endure—what's more, it's self-inflicted.

Emotional Torment Is Worse Than Physical Torment

The truth is that flames and darkness aren't necessary in hell, because emotional pain is far more significant than physical pain. Think about a moment in your life when you were in great physical pain—maybe you once broke a bone or suffered some other injury. Can you really recall the level of pain you were in? No. You may remember it, but the pain has long faded. But I'll bet there is some emotional loss or moment of great regret for you that if someone were to mention it, you could recall every last tremor of that moment. And if you were given the option between choosing to relive that moment and choosing to relive the physical pain,

I'm guessing you would choose the physical pain, hands down, every time.

As I said earlier, I'm a big fan of movies. I love 'em all, but like most guys I have a weak spot for action movies. You make a film about some hero saving the world from bad guys and I'm ready to buy a ticket. I don't care that much if the movie is formulaic as long as the hero kicks butt and takes names. Now I've noticed an interesting thing that happens in a lot of these action movies; maybe you have, too. There's often a scene where the hero is captured by the villain. The hero gets strapped to a chair or a bed where he can't escape, and the villain threatens him with torture unless the hero gives in. But does the hero give in? Of course he doesn't—he's too tough for physical pain to break. And that's when the villain pulls out a secret surprise: he's also captured the hero's wife or girlfriend or partner or child—someone the hero loves deeply. The villain then threatens to torture that person instead. At that point we know the hero is in real trouble. Why? Because the emotional torment of watching someone he loves come to harm is far more painful to the hero than any physical torture the villain can inflict. Wouldn't you feel the same? I'm no tough guy, but if it's a choice between my being hurt and my wife and kids being hurt, I'd give anything to make sure I'm the one in the meat grinder.

So when I say that hell is not a physical torture chamber, I am not saying hell is "not so bad." I'm not saying hell is a place where you can go on ignoring God. Jesus may have used the flames and the worms and the darkness as metaphors, but those metaphors stand for an eternal truth: that hell is a place of utter heartbreak. It is the realization that you have missed the whole point of life.

In Jesus' story of the rich man and Lazarus, Abraham tells the rich man to remember his earthly life. Abraham isn't telling the guy to remember all the fun times so he'll feel better about being in hell. When Abraham points to the rich man's life of wealth and luxury, he's not some friend playing "Remember when?" and laughing over good times. There are no happy memories in hell. The rich man isn't having fond thoughts of his expensive food and his luxurious clothes. He is having haunting memories of how he lived large for frivolous things while excluding the most important thing: God. He is remembering how his life was all about himself and never about others. He is remembering that he could have built a relationship with God, but didn't. He is remembering that he could have shown love to Lazarus, but didn't. Hell is a place of haunting remembrance.

Hell Is a Place of Total Isolation

Mark Twain once quipped, "Heaven for the climate; Hell for the company." But Mark Twain was mistaken. There is no company in hell. Hell is not about relationship; it's about selfishness. Heaven is about relationship. When the rich man looks at paradise, he sees a community. He sees Abraham and Lazarus together, interacting as father and son. But notice there is no mention of anyone hanging out with the rich man. He's by himself. The picture Jesus paints of the rich man's fate is one of total isolation.

People love to joke, "Hell is where all the fun people are. It'll just be a big party. My friends and I will get together and have a grand old time."

Uh, not exactly.

Notice that the rich man isn't eager for his family to join him. In fact, the last thing he wants is for his buddies to wind up in hell. He is alone, in utter anguish, and when his family shows up, they will be alone and in utter anguish as well. There is no "grand old time" to be had. Just separation from God and everyone else. Alone. Forever. That's hell.

Hell Is a Place of Ultimate Understanding

The Bible tells us that when we die, our imperfect knowledge of the world comes to an end. When we close our eyes in this life and open them in the afterlife, something happens to us. We no longer see shadows. We no longer have a limited understanding. We are the desert nomad brought at last to see the ocean for himself. We now know in full: "Now we see things imperfectly as in a cloudy mirror, but then we will see everything with perfect clarity. All that I know now is partial and incomplete, but then I will know everything completely, just as God now knows me completely" (1 Cor. 13:12 NLT).

Paul is saying that when we know in full, and are no longer seeing through shadows, the euphoria of heaven will be heightened. Our understanding then is incomprehensible to us now.

But there's a dark side to that if our destination is hell. Our regret and anguish over having chosen foolishly will be intensified to the final extreme. In hell you cannot hide from your mistakes. You cannot hide from your shame. You cannot pretend you were falsely accused or wronged or treated unfairly, or that you didn't know the truth. Your lies to yourself will be utterly exposed. Your selfishness will be laid bare. Your pretensions will be stripped away. No masks, no covering, no blaming others for your choices or your mistakes. Everything you've ever done to hurt others or reject God will be forever foremost in your mind, unforgotten and unforgiven. And you will know without possibility of contradiction that the simplest choice in the world—to love Christ—would have made all of that go away. That's hell.

Look again at Jesus' description of the rich man's fate. The rich man first calls out for aid from his own anguish. When that doesn't happen, he calls out for help for his family, to keep them away from experiencing that same suffering. Now Jesus doesn't say, but it's not hard to imagine, that such a wealthy man would have a lot of influence over the attitudes of his family and his friends. Everybody wants to be like the rich guy. "Uncle Bill is successful. I want to be like Uncle Bill. Let's do what he did!" So wouldn't part of his pain also be knowing that if his family did follow in his footsteps, they would wind up in hell as well—so it would be his fault as much as theirs? I don't know about you, but if I've done something that causes my wife or kids pain, that hurts me more than anything else.

So what the rich man is suffering is far more than just the torment of being in hell; it's the torment of knowing that he brought it all on himself, and worse, he's misled others that he loves into suffering the same fate. Suddenly, the man who spent his entire life caring only for himself begins to care about others. Thirty seconds after he dies, he comes to ultimate understanding of the purpose of life.

It had nothing to do with his wealth or his home or his suits or his career.

It had everything to do with the beggar outside his gate.

Now he knows. But once you're in hell, *now* is too late.

CHAPTER 19

The Choice

ONE CLAIM OFTEN made in support of atheism is that a loving God couldn't possibly send people to hell. I completely agree. A loving God would never send anyone to hell. And, in fact, God *doesn't* send anyone to hell. People choose to go all on their own.

"What do you mean, people choose to go to hell?" you may be saying. "I wouldn't choose to go there! Nobody sane would choose that."

Sure they would. They do it all the time. You see, there's a catch about eternity. And the catch is this: there are two places to choose from—heaven and hell. And God lives in heaven. So if somebody says they don't want to live with God, well, then, what's left but hell?

Remember when we said that God made us to love us, and wants us to love him back? Remember that we also said love must be a choice?

Well, God is so good that he always allows us to have our choices. If we choose to love God, then he honors that. And if we choose not to love God, he honors that, too.

Tell me, do you want to spend eternity with someone you don't love?

Let's say I offered to give you a fabulous mansion, to supply you with all the money you could want, all the food you desired, everything you could dream of. But I made the stipulation that you had to spend every moment, day and night, with a person you detested. You couldn't get away from them, couldn't take a break from them, had to talk to them. Tell me, would that be your idea of paradise? How do you think that other person would feel about it?

So when people here on earth make it quite clear to God that they want nothing to do with him, what is he supposed to do? Trap them for all eternity with him? Because if you're in heaven, you're with God. Forever and ever. Period.

And God is so good that he refuses to force that experience on anyone who doesn't want it.

If you don't want God, you'll get exactly what you want: no God, in a place where God is not—hell. Because that's the single true quality about hell that we know: God isn't there.

The great theologian and novelist C. S. Lewis said it this way: "The door of hell is locked on the inside."[1] As he put it in another book, "There are only two kinds of people in the end: those who say to God, 'Thy will be done,' and those to whom God says, in the end, '*Thy* will be done.' All that are in Hell, choose it."[2]

One more illustration to prove that point: Let's imagine you were hungry and had nothing to eat for forty days. But every one of those days I came up to you and offered you food—good, healthful food, excellent in every way—and you rejected it. At the end of those forty days, when you died of starvation, would you be just in blaming me for your fate? Of course not. I was trying to feed you; you just turned me down. Your death would be the result of your own choices, not mine.

I've heard claims that asking people to believe in Christ is somehow horribly unfair on the part of God. But where's the logic in that claim? If Christianity's claims are true, that all you have to do to receive God's grace is to ask for it, what is unfair about that? In fact, isn't it far fairer than the other options? Of all the religions, Christianity is the one faith that anybody can fulfill, regardless of ability or status or even age. Say yes to Christ and live. And God puts it out there for you. He says, "Death is coming. But I've prepared an eternity for you, with me, if you're willing to accept my offer. Please accept it; I want you to be with me. But if you don't want that, I'll honor your choice—an eternity without me. You won't like that, but there's nothing I can do to change it. It is what it is. So please choose to be with me."

People get muddled because they don't understand the difference between a threat and a warning. When we warn somebody about the consequences of an action, we aren't being unfair and we aren't threatening them. You can't point at the warning label on a pack of cigarettes and say the surgeon general is threatening you. When your mother told you not to run into the street because a car might hit you, she wasn't threatening you. She was *warning* you about a truth you needed to know.

And that is all I am doing in this chapter, and all God is doing in the Bible. Hell is a truth you need to know about.

Fortunately, so is heaven.

And that's our next chapter.

PART V

Heaven

CHAPTER 20

The Scientist and the Little Boy

"I REGARD THE BRAIN as a computer which will stop working when its components fail. There is no heaven or afterlife for broken-down computers; that is a fairy story for people afraid of the dark." So said Stephen Hawking, Nobel Prize–winning physicist and author.[1]

"Heaven is for real," declared Colton Burpo, an eleven-year-old boy who claims to have visited heaven while undergoing emergency surgery at the age of three.[2]

Wow. Whom do we believe? The celebrated popular scientist or the child? Many people side with Stephen Hawking, and I can understand why. The man is a genius, one of the most brilliant minds in the world today. What he understands about the inner workings of the universe could fill hundreds more books than just the ones he has written. And on the surface, what he says appears to make sense. Heaven, after all, isn't provable. You can't hold up a chunk of heaven and wave it around, or show people photographs of it, or do experiments in a lab to prove its existence. And then, of course, there's the old "It's too good to be true" argument—that it's a little too convenient for a "perfect" world to be just around the corner of death to make up for all the garbage that goes on in this one.

I understand that belief. It's best summed up in the 2009 film *The Invention of Lying*, starring comedian Ricky Gervais. An odd little comedy, it tells the story of a modern-day world almost exactly like ours, with one exception: nobody lies. Nobody has *ever* lied in this world—lying hasn't been invented. So no one questions the truth of what anyone else says. One day, Gervais's character, a down-on-his-luck writer, suddenly "says something that isn't." Soon he has the world at his fingertips, because people automatically believe anything he makes up. If he says he has money in his bank account, the bank assumes their records are wrong. If he claims he hit the jackpot on the slot machine at the local casino, they hand him all their cash. But when he faces the death of his mother, he can't bear to see the fear in her eyes as she contemplates "an eternity of nothingness." So he makes up an afterlife on the spot, to make her last seconds happy.

Unfortunately, the hospital staff overhears him, and word quickly spreads about this new development. Soon people are camped on his lawn, demanding to hear about this place called "heaven." Using empty pizza boxes as his stone tablets, the good-hearted con man invents God, hell, the Ten Commandments (more or less), and a heaven where everybody gets their own mansion and gets to see everyone they've ever loved, as long as they never do more than two "really bad things" on earth. ("Three strikes and you're out.") It's the old Marxist "opiate of the masses" line turned into one big joke.

The Idea of an Afterlife: As Old as Old Can Be

The problem with the story, of course, is that it's based on a line of reasoning that isn't valid on several fronts. First, it assumes that heaven was made up so people would feel good about death. Yet there isn't any evidence that this is the case. Indeed, we don't even know when the concept of an afterlife began. As far as we can tell, belief in an afterlife goes back to the days of prehistoric man. Even cultures with no written language that we know of left signs of elaborate burial rites, which imply a belief in an afterlife. For some of these cultures, we don't even know whether they had complex, abstract language in which to express such ideas as the soul, the afterlife, or heaven. The most they may have communicated were basic instructions to each other regarding tasks, dangers, and human needs. (Which makes the oldest lie probably "Not tonight, dear; I have a headache.")

So, then, who made them up? If belief in an afterlife is inherent to even prelingual human intelligence, as these rites imply, then *no one* made it up. There was no "big liar" to tell the "big lie." Human beings expect an afterlife because that expectation is innate to us.

Remember in chapter 5 how we discussed the universality of belief in an afterlife? Heaven falls under that same umbrella. Throughout history, all civilized cultures have expressed belief in a heaven. Even cultures that we consider primitive have shared similar concepts. (By the way, I freely acknowledge that belief in a heaven such as I describe is probably *not* innate. But then, neither is belief in other concepts, such as freedom and human rights, yet we accept these as inherent truths.)

So let's look back at Hawking's claim. Does he offer any proof for this statement? No. Does he offer any evidence for it? No. Comparing the brain to a computer isn't evidence; it's an analogy. But a brain isn't a computer. It's not just a device for calculation, nor is it equipped with software. In fact, there is very little similarity between a computer and a human brain, aside from our tendency to say that computers "think," which computers actually do not do. The truth is, no computer can generate spontaneous thought. Yet you and I do this all the time.

So Hawking's analogy comparing a brain to a computer is fundamentally flawed. He has compared two superficially similar objects and concluded they are equivalents. It's a bit like saying ice cream and pie are both desserts, therefore ice cream is pie, when in fact they are different in every way. (And I'll have both, please.)

But as we've already established, the assumption that who we are is simply our brains and nothing else is not a valid assumption. We are more than a brain or a body; we are a soul as well. In the end, Hawking's statement in this interview contains neither fact nor evidence but merely speculation. So Hawking's argument isn't valid. It may be a statement of his personal belief, but it holds no more logical weight than Colton Burpo's.

What about Hawking's fairy-tale accusation, or the "wishful thinking" argument? This is the one presented in *The Invention of Lying*. It's the argument that heaven is too good to be true. It implies that heaven is supposed to be a place where everybody's rich and happy and lives in their own heavenly version of the Kennedy compound; it sounds so preposterous that it must be wishful thinking that exists to make poor people feel better about death. But as we'll see, that's not what heaven is like at all, at least not from the biblical perspective. It doesn't fit in with the various heavens believed in by non-Christian cultures, much less Christian teachings.

The only possible validity of the "too good to be true" argument is to call us to examine the reality of heaven, not to reject its existence.

The Burpo Perspective

So what about Colton Burpo? Colton is the son of Todd Burpo, a part-time pastor, business owner, and volunteer fireman and coach from the small farming town of Imperial, Nebraska. The best-selling book *Heaven Is for Real* tells the story of the family's unexpected plunge into a parent's nightmare, when the very young Colton suffered a burst appendix. The time was a trial to the family in every way, and a test of the father's faith. But a few months after it was all over, and the family was settling back into as much normalcy as they could, Colton made a surprise announcement. When asked if he remembered the hospital, the now four-year-old replied, "Yes. That's where the angels sang to me." This surprised his parents, as no one had been singing anything during his entire stay. The family treated it as just an interesting comment until Colton added, "Jesus had the angels sing to me because I was so scared. They made me feel better. . . . I sat in Jesus' lap." The not-yet-preschooler then went on to describe an out-of-body experience in which he watched the doctor working on him, saw his mother, Sonjia, praying and talking on her cell phone, and his father praying in "a little room."[3]

During the operation, Todd Burpo had indeed taken refuge in a small, unused room, where he not only prayed but also flat-out raged at God over his son's life-threatening condition. Not even Sonjia knew where he had been.

That was not the end of Colton's story. Over the next several months, without prompting, Colton would share more details of his experience, including meeting Todd's grandfather, who had died years before Colton was born and whom Colton knew nothing about. At last, Todd determined to question Colton about what had happened, being careful not to lead or suggest anything, and letting Colton answer at his own pace. What came out was astounding.

Colton described a place "where all the colors are," that had animals and "lots of kids." In simple language he talked of seeing "red markers" on Jesus' hands and feet (though Colton had never been taught about the Crucifixion), of being given "wings" ("Though mine weren't very big"), of meeting God and another sister (Sonjia had miscarried a previous pregnancy, which Colton had never been told about and Sonjia never discussed), and even of staying with his great-grandfather "Pop." (When shown a picture of "Pop" in his late sixties, Colton didn't know who it was. But without any prompting, he immediately identified a photograph of a twenty-nine-year-old Pop as being the man he met.) One of the biggest surprises came when Colton informed his father that God was "three people"—God, Jesus, and the Holy Spirit—even though the four-year-old had no previous concept of the Trinity. (It certainly wasn't part of the Sunday-school curriculum at their church, which Todd and Sonjia, as pastor and head of the children's program respectively, knew very well.)[4]

Now children can imagine all sorts of things, and pick up conversations we don't know they hear. But Colton's impulse to share his account wasn't the result of his parents encouraging him to talk about heaven. It was only after Colton had spontaneously mentioned things on several separate occasions that his father decided to ask questions—and even then, only when Colton brought up the matter first, usually with a surprising detail on a subject he had no reason to know at all. Those details, like Pop, the miscarried sister, his father's location in the hospital, and the triune nature of God (which even ministers have a tough time grasping), finally convinced his parents that Colton's experiences were very real indeed.

In the debate between a guileless three-year-old who experienced heaven and a Nobel Prize–winning physicist who's only speculating, I have to lay the weight on the side of the three-year-old. As the prophet wrote, "And a little child shall lead them" (Isa. 11:6).

Science and Heaven

I don't want to get too much into this because it can get a little heady, but despite Hawking's speculations, science actually supports the general concept of heaven. As we examined the evidence for God, we saw that current theories in physics put forth the idea that dimensions exist outside of the reality we know and experience. Even theories that reject the notion of such dimensions still revolve around some concept of an external reality that contains the universe and exists independent of time itself. Aren't these among the qualities of heaven: external to our universe and eternal as well?

We also saw that God is external to the universe and eternal in nature. If that is the case, then where does God exist, except in an external, eternal realm? Just as God is eternal, his realm must also be. Last, we established that God is good and perfect, which implies that the realm he lives in would also be good and perfect.

So we have a realm, if you will, that is external to our universe, eternal and out of time, good and perfect, and the *dwelling place* (for lack of better words) of God.

I believe the word for that place is *heaven.*

It's not too good to be true. It's too good to *not* be true.

CHAPTER 21

Chubby Cherubs Playing Harps?

NOW I'M NOT going to tell you that we don't have an imaginary heaven. We do. We have all sorts of them, imagined by all sorts of people, for all sorts of reasons.

For example, when I say "heaven" to you, what are you most likely to picture?

You probably think of a place up in the sky, full of big, fluffy clouds you can stand on. You probably think of people who have wings like angels or who have become angels since they died, and little chubby cherubs (with or without Pampers) who go around playing harps. You may think of people dressed in white or choir robes who spend eternity singing hymns as part of a church service that goes on forever and ever. (I don't know about you, but I've been in some church services that have lasted forever, and at no point was I thinking, *This is heaven!*)

Well, those are the crazy images our movies and stained-glass windows and even our churches have given us about heaven. But is the heaven we imagine the heaven that is real? Is that the heaven that Jesus spoke of or that the Bible describes?

Some people may tell you that what heaven is like isn't all that important as long as you go there. They have a point, but isn't it more appealing to have some idea of what to expect? When I go on vacation, I like to know that my vacation site is going to be a nice place. So I look at brochures or search the Internet to see what I'm getting. A name's not enough. Take the White Sands National Monument: if you don't read up on it, you might pack for a beach only to arrive and find out it's a desert.

The Bible even tells us to prepare for heaven. "Since you have been raised to new life with Christ, set your sights on the realities of heaven" (Col. 3:1 NLT).

God wants us to have a handle on the heavenly realities. He doesn't expect us to go blindly. He wants us to know the truth. And the truth can be summed up with the answers to two questions: What is heaven? What is heaven like? We'll tackle the first question in this chapter.

What Is Heaven?

Heaven Is Where God Lives and Rules

The Bible makes it clear that heaven is both God's dwelling place and his throne (1 Kings 8:30; Isa. 66:1–2). Jesus calls it "the kingdom of heaven." There is no such thing as a kingdom without a king. God lives in heaven. God rules in heaven. These two qualities are intertwined and inseparable. Where God dwells, *everything* happens according to his will. Would you expect it to be any different? In God's house, God rules.

Heaven Is a Real Place

We've already established this truth when we looked at the evidence for God (and for heaven), but it's worth restating. Heaven is a real place. It's not just something we feel when we meditate and hum odd little mantras. Nor is it a philosophical construct, or some ethereal realm of vague lights and fuzzy *Star Trek* effects. Heaven is a real place.

Jesus insisted on the reality of heaven. When talking to his disciples, he said, "In my Father's house are many rooms; if it were not so, I would have told you. I am going there to prepare a place for you" (John 14:2 NIV).

Those are emphatic, definite words. It could be paraphrased as "Look, guys, I'm telling it to you straight. If I were just making this all up, I'd have said so." Jesus is making it quite clear that he isn't just trying to make everybody feel better about death. He's not talking about good memories of dead people or some philosophical concept. He means a real, tangible place that God has prepared for you and me. And that's his next point.

God Made Heaven for Us

When we looked at hell, we learned that hell was not made for us. We learned that it was intended for the devil and his angels. It was never meant for people, and if people go there, it's simply because they choose to, not because God wants them to. But God did make a place for people. That place is heaven. And God planned for it all along.

Jesus said that God prepared heaven from the very beginning: "Then the King will say to those on his right, 'Come, you who are blessed by my Father; take your inheritance, the kingdom prepared for you since the creation of the world'" (Matt. 25:34 NIV).

What kingdom was prepared for you at the creation of the world? Heaven. Jesus was saying that when God spoke the universe into existence, at that very time God began to plan heaven for us. God knew we weren't destined to live on earth for long. He knew we would each have seventy, eighty, maybe even a hundred years at the most, and then we would die. Our spirits would leave our bodies and live on into eternity. The place he prepared for our spirits is heaven. It's the eternal home God made for us.

CHAPTER 22

Beyond Our Wildest Imagination

I KNOW WHAT YOU'RE thinking: *What's heaven going to be like?* That's what we want to know. What are we going to see and do when we get there? Everybody wants to hear that.

Let's start by acknowledging that in many ways heaven may be indescribable. I believe some of the details about heaven were intentionally left out of the Bible. Not because God doesn't want us to know, but because some things about heaven are too big and too amazing for us to comprehend. Heaven is too incredible for us to conceive. "No eye has seen, no ear has heard, no mind has conceived what God has prepared for those who love him" (1 Cor. 2:9 NIV). Despite how complex our brains are, none of them, not even a brain as brilliant as Stephen Hawking's, can begin to imagine how wonderful heaven will be. There is nothing on earth to compare it to.

That's the first truth about what heaven is like.

HEAVEN IS MIND-BLOWING

Have you ever had a moment in life you wished would last forever? You're going through life, and you get into one of those moments when all the stress is gone. You're wrapped up in it. You're not thinking about anything else—you're just enjoying that moment. For me, those moments come when I'm with Lisa and the kids, and we're swimming in the pool or on vacation somewhere or maybe just hanging out together. I love those moments. I wish they would last forever.

Think about that moment for you. Wouldn't you like to bottle it and keep it? Wouldn't you like to live it over and over again? It's that moment when, if you could, you'd spend anything at all just to have that moment continue, because you're convinced that it can't get any better than this.

The truth is, yes, it can.

If you take that moment and multiply it by infinity, only then can you begin to see what heaven will be like. How do I know this? Because of the verse we just read: "No mind can conceive what God has prepared." Even if I can imagine that perfect moment, multiplied infinite times, I know that my mind *still* hasn't conceived of how good heaven will be.

That's what God does. The Bible puts it this way: "God can do anything, you know—far more than you could ever imagine or guess or request in your wildest dreams!" (Eph. 3:20, *The Message*).

When I think about what heaven should be like, I already know that it is far beyond what I can wrap my little pea brain around. This is the place that God has created for all eternity. If I could define heaven in just a few words, or even a thousand words, or a whole book of words, it wouldn't be heaven. Heaven is a product of *God's* imagination, not mine. In order for heaven to be heaven, it can't be definable in human terms. Heaven has to be outside of us. It has to be more than us. We have this picture in our minds of pearly gates and streets of gold and all these things, but I think when we get to heaven, our eyes are going to be wider than baseballs and our mouths will be able to hold a thousand melons, so great will be our astonishment at what heaven is actually like.

Have you ever tried to explain to somebody who doesn't have kids what it's like the moment you see your kid for the first time?

They nod as if they know, but they don't. If you want to know that they don't, try describing the delivery experience to them. Tell them how mind-blowing it is when the kid's head pops out, and watch their polite expressions freeze. Tell them about the joy of cutting the umbilical cord, and notice the pale green hue that starts to creep up their necks. Talk about the baby crying for the very first time and how loud and wonderfully shrill it is, and watch your friends' eyes start looking around the room for an escape route. If you really want to get them, show pictures of your adorable, naked, wet, wrinkly, blue, body-fluid-covered little cutie-pie, and watch them edge toward the door. Finish it off by saying you have a video, and they'll suddenly discover they have an important dentist appointment across town. Yes, at 8 P.M. On a Sunday.

Because the truth of the matter is that nobody appreciates what the birth moment is like except those who have been through it themselves. Nobody understands the joy and the indescribable awe that comes with the arrival of a baby except those who have been there.

But when that same couple has their first child, suddenly they get it. Suddenly, they're ready to agree with you that nothing could be more beautiful or wonderful. Suddenly, they understand.

When I saw my daughter, Nicole, for the first time, I learned what that experience is like. Before she was born, I was in the delivery room with Lisa, and it was horrible. Lisa was screaming in pain. She was holding on to my hand so tightly I had lost circulation. I tried to crack a joke to lighten her up. Bad move. She went from screaming in pain to screaming at me. I was thinking, *This is the worst experience on the whole planet! Lisa's in pain, my hand is numb, and somehow it's all become my fault. Why did I agree to be in here?*

And then, all of a sudden, Nicole was born.

At that moment a rush of joy went through me unlike any I had ever known. I laughed and cried, all at the same time. Lisa was laughing and crying with me, or maybe I was laughing and crying with her. It didn't matter. In that instant, all of the pain, all of the tough days of the pregnancy just disappeared. We were completely overcome with joy.

That's what heaven will be like when we experience it for the first time, magnified by a million.

Paul once described an experience he had with heaven:

> I was caught up to the third heaven fourteen years ago. Whether I was in my body or out of my body, I don't know—only God knows. Yes, only God knows whether I was in my body or outside my body. But I do know that I was caught up to paradise and heard things so astounding that they cannot be expressed in words, things no human is allowed to tell. (2 Cor. 12:2–4 NLT)

The term "the third heaven" is interesting, isn't it? What does it mean? Are there three heavens? Maybe Catholic, Protestant, and Confused? No, that's not what it means. Most scholars believe "the third heaven" refers to the place where God resides, the place where the souls of believers go after they die. The first heaven is the earthly atmosphere, what you and I call the sky. The second heaven is the realm of the stars, or outer space. And the third heaven is the dwelling place of God, or paradise. There are other interpretations—for example, that heaven itself is made of layers or tiers—but the majority of scholars believe Paul wasn't describing anything like that, but merely referring to a vision of paradise as a whole.

But the most important part of this statement is the last—that Paul could not put his experience of heaven into words. He couldn't explain it.

We have to realize that not everything in the Bible fits into our neat little labeled boxes. If we could understand God and define him completely, he wouldn't be God. God surpasses our ability to describe him. Some things can't be put into words. God is one. The other is heaven.

But look at the rest of the scripture I quoted earlier: "No eye has seen, no ear has heard, no mind has conceived what God has prepared for those who love him—*but God has revealed it to us by his Spirit*" (1 Cor. 2:9–10 NIV, italics mine).

That second verse makes a big difference, doesn't it? It says that even though we can't know what God has prepared, we have this understanding in our spirit that his heaven is magnificent. Does that mean we know every detail? No. Does it mean we have all the answers? No. But it does mean that God has given us the knowledge that heaven is going to be beyond our wildest imagination.

CHAPTER 23

Our Here Affects Our There

THE APOSTLE PAUL wrote, "We must all appear before the judgment seat of Christ, that each one may receive what is due him for the things done while in the body, whether good or bad" (2 Cor. 5:10 NIV). Most people hear "the judgment seat of Christ" and think it means the Great White Throne of Judgment from Revelation 20—the moment when the dead are judged before God, and God reviews the Book of Life to see who gets to stay in heaven and who does not.

That's not the judgment that Paul describes in 2 Corinthians. The Greek term for this is the *bema seat of judgment*. It's not a term from the law but from athletics. In those days an athletic event would be presided over by a local ruler—a governor, a king, or maybe even Caesar. The ruler would sit in an elevated chair—the *bema seat*—above the stadium, and watch the competition. When the games had ended, the athletes would stand before the ruler and receive their awards for the event based on their performances. The *bema seat* was a seat where rewards were handed out, not punishment.

This life we live on earth is a race, and Jesus himself is presiding over it. He's watching our performance, every moment of the race. And when the race is done, we are going to be rewarded for all the godly things we do.

Heaven Is a Place of Reward

Jesus states this concept of heavenly reward over and over in the Bible.

> Blessed are you when people insult you, persecute you and falsely say all kinds of evil against you because of me. Rejoice and be glad, because great is *your reward* in heaven, for in the same way they persecuted the prophets who were before you. (Matt. 5:11–12 NIV)

> Be careful not to practice your righteousness in front of others before men, to be seen by them. If you do, you will have no *reward from your Father in heaven.* (Matt. 6:1 NIV)

> And if anyone gives a cup of cold water to one of these little ones who is my disciple, truly I tell you, that person will certainly *not lose their reward.* (Matt. 10:42 NIV)

> Rejoice in that day and leap for joy, because *great is your reward in heaven.* For that is how their ancestors treated the prophets. (Luke 6:23 NIV)

> But love your enemies, do good to them, and lend to them without expecting to get anything back. Then *your reward will be great* and you will be children of the Most High, because he is kind to the ungrateful and wicked. (Luke 6:35 NIV)

Paul repeats this idea in his first letter to the Thessalonian church: "After all, what gives us hope and joy, and what will be our proud reward and crown as we stand before our Lord Jesus when he returns? It is you! Yes, you are our pride and joy" (2:19–20 NLT).

What does this mean, when we say heaven is a place of reward? Look again at what Paul said in 2 Corinthians: "So we make it our goal to please him. . . . For we must all appear before the judgment seat of Christ, that each one may receive what is due him for the things done while in the body, good or bad" (5:9–10 NIV).

It means our life goals ought to be to please God, because we are going to stand before him and give accounts of what we have done, good and bad, for him.

So your goal in life ought not to be the biggest house. Your goal in life ought not to be the best job, the fanciest car, where you're going to retire, or how much money you're going to have in the bank. All those things may be wonderful, and God may even choose to bless you with them. But your goal in life ought to be pleasing God. Because someday all the earthly things we invest in with so much of our lives and time are going to pass away. They are going to cease to be important, because all they are is matter. But we are going to live on via our spirits and go into eternity, and there's only going to be one thing that matters—did we please God with our lives?

Heaven is a place of reward.

Heaven Is a Place of Responsibility

Some people think that all we're going to do is bow before the throne of God and sing "Holy, Holy, Holy" into eternity, as if God only knows how to make a looping audio track. Other people think heaven is just going to be an eternal resort where we play golf and tennis and enjoy the never-ending good life. I even know of people who think heaven is going to be an extended wilderness camping trip where we commune with flowers and trees and animals and get piggyback rides from grizzly bears.

I don't know which of those claims appeals to you, but I'm going to have to burst your bubble. Heaven is not an endless repeat of the *Hour of Power*. It is not an eternal copy of The Villages retirement resort in Florida. And it's not a High Sierra adventure weekend.

Are we going to do some of that? Maybe, maybe not. Revelation describes a general celebration when Christ is presented as King of Kings, but nowhere does the Bible say that moment is going to continue forever. No, the truth is, heaven is neither a church service nor a vacation. Heaven is a place of responsibility. Yes, that's right—in heaven we'll have work to do.

Remember Colton Burpo, the little boy who visited heaven? In one of the early conversations with his father, Colton announced, "Jesus gave me work to do. That was my favorite part of Heaven."[1] Colton never said what his work was, but doesn't it sound like a strange pronouncement for a kid's version of heaven? Having "work" to do and calling it his "favorite" part?

Again, kids can imagine all sorts of things. But in the parable of the talents in Matthew 25, Jesus makes an interesting statement about heaven, and it's so important that he says it twice. If you don't know the story, it goes something like this:

Heaven is like a wealthy man who has to go out of town on an important journey. So he calls in his top three money managers and hands them each a share of his current portfolio, "each according to his ability" (Matt. 25:15 NIV). One manager gets $5 million to handle, one gets $2 million, and the other $1 million.

The first two are real go-getters. They rush out, start making investments left and right, and in short order double their boss's portfolio. But the last guy is a coward. He just buries the money in a suitcase in his backyard.

When the boss gets back, he calls the three in and asks them to present his profits. When the first announces his amazing success, their boss is ecstatic and says, "Well done, good and faithful servant! You have been faithful with a few things; I will put you in charge of many things. Come and share your master's happiness!" (Matt. 25:21 NIV). And when the second manager reveals that he, too, has made a handsome profit, the master repeats the praise in exactly the same way.

The story goes on to reveal how the boss reacts to the cowardly manager, but for now I want to focus on that twice-repeated statement of praise, particularly the second sentence: "You have been faithful with a few things; I will put you in charge of many things."

The boss doesn't say, "Now you can retire a wealthy man with a great pension and never work again." Instead, he gives each manager even *more* responsibility than he had before—in fact, he *doubles it.*

At the end of the story, the boss turns his wrath on the cowardly, lazy manager and orders that the $1 million now be given to the first servant. The boss cries out: "Everyone who has will be given more, and he will have an abundance" (Matt. 25:29 NIV).

Now where do these new responsibilities take place? Well, remember how the story starts—"The kingdom of heaven is like . . ." The story is about heaven; therefore the new responsibilities the master awards to his servants take place in heaven, not on earth. Heaven is a place of responsibility.

How you handle your job here matters eternally. How you handle your money here matters eternally. How you treat your husband, your wife, your children, your coworkers—it all matters eternally. And it matters for all of eternity because what we do here determines the responsibilities we will get there. That's why the Bible says, "Whatever you do, work at it with all your heart, as working for the Lord, not for men" (Col. 3:23 NIV). What you do matters for eternity.

What you do when you think nobody else is checking you out matters, because even if no one else can see what you do, God can. God is watching you and asking himself, *What responsibilities can I give this person for all of eternity?*

Heaven is not going to be an eternal church service. Heaven is not going to be a vacation resort. Heaven is not going to be a cosmic petting zoo. Heaven is going to be a place of responsibility—yours.

CHAPTER 24

Our Dream and God's Dream

HEAVEN IS A place where there will be "none of that." You're probably wondering what I mean by that. None of what? Well, let's take a look at what the Bible says about it:

> Now I saw a new heaven and a new earth, for the first heaven and the first earth had passed away. Also there was no more sea. Then I, John, saw the holy city, New Jerusalem, coming down out of heaven from God, prepared as a bride adorned for her husband. And I heard a loud voice from heaven saying, "Behold, the tabernacle of God is with men, and He will dwell with them, and they shall be His people. God Himself will be with them and be their God. And God will wipe away every tear from their eyes; there shall be no more death, nor sorrow, nor crying. There shall be no more pain, for the former things have passed away."
>
> Then He who sat on the throne said, "Behold, I make all things new." And He said to me, "Write, for these words are true and faithful." (Rev. 21:1–5 NKJV)

Now you know what I mean when I say heaven is a place where there will be "none of that." None of the things in life that cause us pain. None of the things that hold us back. None of the things that keep us from life as we're supposed to live it.

Poverty—none of that!
Hunger—none of that!
Disease—none of that!
Divorce—none of that!
Betrayal—none of that!
Worry—none of that!
Fear—none of that!
Grief—none of that!
Sadness—none of that!
Hate—none of that!

Look at the promise again: "And God will wipe away every tear from their eyes; there shall be no more death, nor sorrow, nor crying. There shall be no more pain, for the former things have passed away. Then He who sat on the throne said, 'Behold, I make all things new.' And He said to me, 'Write, for these words are true and faithful.'"

Jesus wants us to know this so much that he says it flat out. He tells us we can take it to the bank. We can base all our lives and dreams and hopes on his words. God has made heaven everything that he intended life to be.

You see, this world is not the place that God rules; heaven is. God doesn't rule the earth. Paul says, "Satan . . . is the god of this world" (2 Cor. 4:4 NLT). He's referring to the devil, who is called the ruler of this world. God doesn't rule here. God is in ultimate control, just like the bus driver is in ultimate control of the school bus. But if you've ever ridden in the back of a school bus, you know the bus driver certainly does not rule what happens on the bus. If he did, no little boy would pull some little girl's hair. If he did, no bully would pick on a kid with glasses. If he did, nobody would scrawl a rude word on the back of a seat.

Don't misunderstand me—God is definitely in control. He has the final say. But he is not ruling every detail on the earth today. Where God rules, there is "none of that." And all of us know this world is overrun with far too much of the "that"! This is not the place God wanted us to be.

But heaven will be.

Heaven Is a Place Where We See God Face-to-Face

Look again at the passage from Revelation, particularly the third verse: "And I heard a loud voice from heaven saying, 'Behold, the tabernacle of God is with men, and He will dwell with them, and they shall be His people. God Himself will be with them and be their God.'"

This is one of the most amazing promises in the Bible. When we are in heaven we will see God face-to-face. We will even *live* with him.

I don't know about you, but I don't like having a conversation with somebody when I can't see them. When I talk to somebody, I like to be face-to-face. I like to look people in the eyes. Imagine living with someone you love and never being able to see them.

But why is it so amazing that we will see God face-to-face? To understand why, we need to look at the story of Moses.

You know the basic story. God announces that he wants Moses to lead the children of Israel out of Egypt and into the promised land. God allows Moses to perform miracles and sends the plagues and gives Moses the Ten Commandments. But that's not enough for Moses. Suddenly, he's scared that right in the middle of things God is going to just run off and leave him high and dry. So he demands a sign from God, to prove that God intends to stay with Moses. They go back and forth a bit (with God being remarkably patient) until Moses comes up with an idea that will satisfy his nerves and his curiosity. He asks God to show himself.

Here's the rest of the conversation:

> Then Moses said, "Now show me your glory."
>
> And the Lord said, "I will cause all my goodness to pass in front of you, and I will proclaim my name, the Lord, in your presence. I will have mercy on whom I will have mercy, and I will have compassion on whom I will have compassion. But," he said, "you cannot see my face, for no one may see me and live." (Exod. 33:18–20 NIV)

In the Old Testament, the presence of God was so guarded that no one except the priest could go into the innermost chamber, the "holy of holies," in the temple. When the priest went in, he had a long rope around his waist that stuck out through the temple curtain. Why? Because the Jews believed that the priest might accidentally see God and die on the spot, and they would have to drag the body back out with the rope. Seeing God's face was hazardous to one's earthly health.

But heaven is a place where there is no more rope! We can go into God's presence and behold him face-to-face. That means more than just seeing him in his physical beauty. It means finally getting to see God for who he is. The Bible says, "For now we see only a reflection as in a mirror; then we shall see face to face. Now I know in part; then I shall know fully, even as I am fully known" (1 Cor. 13:12 NIV).

What will we fully know? We will finally know God for who he really is. We will finally see him as . . .

> our healer
> our provider
> our hope
> our all in all
> our more than enough
> our life
> our breath
> our Creator
> our righteousness

our justifier
our Friend
our Father
our King
our peace
our joy
our Deliverer
our salvation
our Redeemer

The key to experiencing life more fully is to know God more fully. The more you know God here on earth, the more fully you live. But in heaven you won't simply know more—you'll know *all*. You will know everything God is. And because you'll know all, you'll live life to the fullest—the life God intended for you when he made you—because you will fully understand why he made you, down to the last desire of your heart.

Heaven is the place where you will see him face-to-face.

Heaven Is the Place Where God's Dreams Come True

I love spending time with my kids. Whether it's together or one-on-one, to me nothing is better. My son, Joseph, will call me at work and say, "Dad, when can we go to the batting cage?" When I pull into the garage, he'll be waiting there with his baseball stuff on—I don't even have time to go inside.

One afternoon I got off from work early, which meant I got to pick Joseph up from school. I thought this would be a great moment for some father-son time, so when he got in the car, I said, "Joe, do you want to go to the batting cage with me?"

To my surprise, he looked at me and said, "Dad, my friend said he was going to call me when he got home from school. I want to wait for my friend to call."

I was just crushed. I thought, *He's ditching me for his friend!*

I said, "Well, Mom can take the call, and she'll tell him you'll call him back."

"No, I really want to wait for his call."

I thought, *You're choosing to spend time with your friend over me?*

Now I'm best buds with my son. I call him "my little buddy." I tease him and say, "When you get older, are you still going to be best friends with your dad?" "Who's your best pal?" "Who do you want to hang out with, your buddies or your dad?"

And he'd always say back, "I want to hang out with you, Dad."

But that day he said, "I want to wait for the phone call."

And I was heartbroken. That wasn't the afternoon I had dreamed of.

It's like that on earth. We fit God in whenever we don't have something better to do. We think we'll squeeze him in when we don't have a family wedding, work, a ball game, or the lawn to mow. Whatever task is in front of us, we'll just throw God a few minutes when it's done . . . if something else doesn't come up.

Sometimes I think God is looking at us on earth and thinking, *You're ditching me for all of the cares of the world?*

But when we get to heaven, God is going to get to have uninterrupted time with us. That's his dream. That's why he created the earth, so he could have fellowship with us. Look at Revelation again: "And I heard a loud voice from heaven saying, 'Behold, the tabernacle of God is with men, and He will dwell with them, and they shall be His people. God Himself will be with them and be their God.'"

That's what God has always wanted.

Usually we think of heaven as the place where all our dreams come true. It is, but more than that, it's the place where all of God's dreams come true. God's dream is this: to have unbroken fellowship with us.

Remember how it all got started? Back in the Garden of Eden, the Bible tells us that God would come down to walk in the garden to spend time with Adam and Eve. Can you imagine?

Hanging with God? Walking around with him, talking about everything? It must have been amazing. But what happened? "Then the man and his wife heard the sound of the Lord God as he was walking in the garden in the cool of the day, and they hid from the Lord God among the trees of the garden" (Gen. 3:8 NIV).

The fellowship was broken.

God's dream is to bring it back.

If you want to know what God's dream is,

- ask the parents who have just dropped off their kid at college for the first time
- ask the father who lifts the veil from his daughter's face and kisses her on the cheek before he gives her away to another man
- ask the mother of the soldier who goes off to war

God's dream is to spend eternity in unbroken fellowship with you and me, forever.

Heaven is the place where that finally happens.

It is the place where God's dream comes true.

CHAPTER 25

What About Kids and Animals?

THERE ARE ALL sorts of other things that people want to know about heaven. Most of these are things about which we can only guess.

ARE THERE ANIMALS IN HEAVEN?

The Bible doesn't say. It does, of course, mention the wolf lying down with the lamb (Isa. 11:6), but whether that's supposed to be a real wolf and a real lamb or a metaphor for peace is up to interpretation. But I think it's significant that Revelation 21 makes a point of mentioning both a "new heaven and a new earth." There are also descriptions of rivers and trees (Rev. 22: 1–2). To me that implies a physical realm like this one, only perfect as God intended. So I would expect to see animals in heaven, though I'm just speculating.

ARE THERE CHILDREN IN HEAVEN?

I have to say yes, because of the special place God has in his heart for kids. Jesus made a point of stopping what he was doing whenever children were brought to him. He even lectured the disciples when they tried to shoo away a group of kids because they didn't want them to bother the Lord: "Jesus said, 'Let the little children come to me, and do not hinder them, for the kingdom of heaven belongs to such as these'" (Matt. 19:14 NIV). That seals the deal for me. Colton Burpo is right—heaven has lots of kids.

Another question is whether they grow up in heaven. I don't know. While getting old is certainly in the "no more of that" category, I don't know what God has arranged about it in heaven. Anything I say would be speculation. But I do know that the middle school years would be a lot easier to handle in heaven than they are on earth.

Will We Recognize Our Loved Ones?

Yes. If you'll recall, when we talked about the soul we mentioned how the disciples immediately recognized the spirits of Elijah and Moses when they appeared to talk with Jesus (Matt. 17:1–8). If the disciples could recognize two people they had never met, I think it's safe to say we will certainly recognize the people we know and love from life.

Will We Have Mansions?

Nobody knows. In the verse "In My Father's house are many mansions" (John 14:2 NKJV), the word translated as "mansions" literally means "rooms." In Jesus' day, before a young man married his bride, he and his father would build an additional bedchamber onto the family home. This new room would be for the young couple, and they would move in with the groom's family. Jesus' description, then, is of a house that has many rooms for the new family members coming in.

Does that mean we'll all be living in some huge house? Again, I don't know. But I think Jesus is using metaphor to make a point. For example, I come from a large Italian family. Italians love family. It's part of our tradition to want everybody living in one home. When my mother and father were first married, they moved in with my grandparents, and so did my uncle. My grandparents loved it. If my grandpa could have kept building rooms onto the house and adding more family members, he would have! As it was, when I was growing up I lived in a duplex, and the family next door was my aunt, uncle, and cousins, which for us was practically the same as having everybody in one big house.

I see God that way: he wants all his family together with him, and he's got enough rooms for all of us. Whether those rooms are rooms or mansions or something else, I don't know. We'll just have to find out when we get there. But whatever our dwelling place is, it will be beyond our wildest imagination.

The last question, though, is really the big one. We'll tackle that one in our next section.

PART VI

Me: How Should Eternity Affect My Now?

CHAPTER 26

All About You

I SAW A YOUNG girl wearing a T-shirt the other day that proudly declared IT'S ALL ABOUT ME! I don't know if she got the joke or not—she was probably too young even to read it. But having a daughter, I certainly got a smile from it. (And it's not just daughters who could wear that shirt, by the way.) From the time they're born, children do seem to think the world revolves around them. Of course, I can't say that we improve much on things as adults. I know I've said enough "I wants" just in the last day to make one think that I expect the universe to serve my bidding. How about you?

Oddly, we act as if this is a new attitude on the planet. Pundits and finger waggers love to criticize the Me Generation, as if everyone walking around today just suddenly adopted that girl's T-shirt as their personal motto. As if no one in the history of the planet had ever had that same concept.

But Jesus knew better. He knew that the Me Generation began with Adam and Eve and continued without stop. He told a story about the ultimate "Me" person:

> The ground of a certain rich man yielded an abundant harvest. He thought to himself, "What shall I do? I have no place to store my crops."
>
> Then he said, "This is what I'll do. I will tear down my barns and build bigger ones, and there I will store my surplus grain. And I'll say to myself, 'You have plenty of grain

> laid up for many years. Take life easy; eat, drink and be merry.'"
>
> But God said to him, "You fool! This very night your life will be demanded from you. Then who will get what you have prepared for yourself?"
>
> This is how it will be with whoever stores up things for themselves but is not rich toward God. (Luke 12:16–21 NIV)

Hmmm. Sound like anyone you know?

Look at the man in the story and how he talks: "What shall *I* do?" "This is what *I'll* do." "*I* will." "*I'll* say to *myself*." How more me-centered can you get?

But you can bet Jesus' listeners recognized that guy. I can imagine each guy in the crowd glancing at the guy next to him, thinking, *Oh, yeah, that's him, all right,* without noticing that the guy on the other side was looking and thinking the same thing. Me Generation, first century.

Before you say, "Oh, yes, that's true," you might recall that I've already retold this story in modern terms. It's the one at the beginning of this book, featuring a wealthy businessman instead of a farmer. It doesn't matter if the guy is a farmer, a businessman, a banker, a real-estate tycoon, or for that matter the best-dressed desperate housewife on the block. It's the "Me" attitude in all of us that is the issue—then and now.

And the point Jesus was trying to make is what eternity means to his listeners.

Don't Make Yourself a Fool

Think again about that story. Was the guy good at his business? Apparently so; he amassed a big profit. Was he responsible in a financial sense? Well, even by today's standards, we have to say yes; he examined his resources and planned for his future. In fact, this guy had a retirement plan in mind even before such a thing existed. We can imagine this guy talking it out with his financial adviser, structuring how he was going to avoid the taxes, how he was going to provide for day-to-day expenses, maybe even working up a solid emergency fund: every wise financial thing we do today. He was planning for every future, except one.

He didn't plan for death.

He didn't plan for eternity.

In all his planning for the rest of his life, he missed the whole point of life. And for that God called him a fool. The rest was all just a wash.

To be a fool in God's eyes is to miss the point of life.

You've probably heard the old Stephen Covey mantra that the main thing is to keep the main thing the main thing. Well, according to God, the main thing of life is to prepare for death or, rather, to prepare for *real* life—the life beyond the grave. To do otherwise is to be a fool.

Will you be a fool?

Or will you accept the challenge of eternity?

Whatever decision you make, it's going to be all about you. Just not in the way you used to think.

CHAPTER 27

Monopoly Money

IN THE PARABLE we just read, God didn't call the man a fool because he was wealthy. There are a lot of wealthy men and women in the Bible: Abraham, David, Solomon. Many scholars today believe that Jesus' ministry was in part funded by a wealthy woman named Joanna, who was married to King Herod's steward. And God didn't call the man a fool for making careful plans about his wealth.

God called the man a fool because he had built his life around his possessions. He planned without thinking about God, and even more than that, without thinking about eternity. He built his whole life on stuff that didn't matter.

THE NAME OF THE GAME

I love the game Monopoly. I think it's in my nature—my dad was an accountant, after all, and all that wheeling and dealing and adding up funds just appeals to me. As you know, Monopoly comes with great amounts of brightly colored paper money, in large denominations. By the end of the game you can wind up with staggering sums. But what would you think of someone who tried to take that money into a store to buy groceries? You'd think the guy was nuts. "Monopoly money is only good in the game," you'd say. And you'd be right. Trying to use Monopoly money outside the game is foolish, because Monopoly money has no real significance.

I think you can see my point here.

When we live our lives as though we're playing Monopoly, we amass all this stuff that seems to have significance in our world. The world tells us we've won something big, but the truth is, it's just a silly little game. We can't take earthly money and do anything with it in eternity. It has no significance there. You can show up on God's doorstep and point back to your amazing portfolio with the million-dollar balance sheet and the incredible retirement plan, and God will treat it the same way your corner grocer would treat a handful of Monopoly money: "Your currency is no good here. Try somewhere else."

You have to build your life on what matters eternally.

When I was a young man, I, too, had a plan. I was going to be a CPA attorney. I was going to get rich. I was going to get married. I was going to set myself up on easy street. I told myself I had one up on the rich fool. I was a Christian; I'd read the parable. But, you see, I had decided to include God in my plans, but only on my own terms. I had felt God's call into the ministry. I knew what he wanted me to do, and I knew that I wanted to do it. But since I also knew (or thought) that ministers were always poor, I thought I'd trump that by getting rich first and then doing ministry as sort of a "second half of life" thing.

Nowadays I have a funny feeling that God was listening to all my plans and just quietly laughing.

But he let me go through college and get my accounting degree. He let me take a job at one of the most prestigious CPA firms in New Jersey. He let Lisa and me start building a new house for when we got married. And he let me get good and miserable chasing after my own plan. And that's when he said, "I want you to quit all that and become a minister for four hundred dollars a month."

Did I mention the new house?

At the time, Lisa and I were looking at a potential combined income of $65,000, and that was back in 1994 when we were both under twenty-two years old. To me that was a huge jump-start on the American dream—my American dream. I argued with God about that. I pointed out to him all my careful planning. I told him that he had not seen fit to explain to me just where that $400-a-month minister's job was going to lead, that it had absolutely no future or financial viability. I couldn't buy groceries for $400 a month, much less pay for a house or even a decent apartment. In short, I was waving my Monopoly money around while forgetting that heaven uses gold bricks as pavement.

God was trying to teach me not to be a fool. God was saying, "All that stuff you are beginning to build your life on—the fancy career, the fancy house, the fancy job title—it's just Monopoly money. It's worthless to me. You need to build your life on something that will matter eternally, and I'm giving you that chance. Trust me."

So I did. I gave up the accountant's income, the law-school plans, and the fancy new house, and took on the role of assistant pastor for $400 a month, living in my in-laws' basement. I gave it all up to follow God's plan for me. And to date, God's plan for my life (as it always is) has been far more wonderful and blessed than I could ever have imagined. And to boot, I know this: I'm building my life on what matters eternally.

How about you? Are you ready to stop chasing after Monopoly money and get in the real game?

Store Up Treasures in Heaven

The story of the rich fool isn't the only place where Jesus brought up the idea. In his Sermon on the Mount, Jesus expanded on this theme: "Do not lay up for yourselves treasures on earth, where moth and rust destroy and where thieves break in and steal; but lay up for yourselves treasures in heaven, where neither moth nor rust destroys and where thieves do not break in and steal. For where your treasure is, there your heart will be also" (Matt. 6:19–21 NKJV).

It's pretty clear here that Jesus is pointing out the rich man's folly again. He's saying flat out, "All those bank accounts, stock portfolios, retirement plans, and whatnot that you've been planning and figuring and investing in all these years—you know what? They're not going to last. The bank will fail, the stock will plummet, the retirement plan will turn out to be a Ponzi scheme. Poof! They'll be gone. And in the end, you'll just find out they were so much Monopoly money. If you want to make a lasting investment, you need to look to God's bank account. Put your treasure there, and it will never vanish. And you'll be the better for it."

So how do we make those kinds of investments?

Live to Die

I'll bet that title made you stop. "Live to die? What do you mean by that, Frank?" Well, I don't mean dressing like you're headed for your own funeral. And I certainly don't mean acting like it. I've known some people who couldn't talk about anything but death or whatever was going to bring it about for them this week. Those people are miserable, and miserable to be around. They're living to be dead. I'm not talking about that.

When I say "Live to die," what I mean is live so that you are prepared for eternity. Live with the understanding that life doesn't end when you die—it actually all begins. This life is preparation for the next one. And what matters there is far different from what matters here. That's why we need to relearn how to live. In the words of Jesus, we need to live rich toward God. How do we do that?

We need to *live now.*

We need to *live legacy.*

We need to *live people.*

We need to *live loved.*

There is no time to waste. Eternity waits for no man. So don't procrastinate. In this moment, decide to live now.

CHAPTER 28

Live Now

YOU'VE PROBABLY HEARD the saying, "Eat, drink, and be merry, for tomorrow we may die." Now you know where it came from, at least in part. It's a corruption of what Jesus said in the story of the rich fool. The rich man said to himself, "You have plenty of grain laid up for many years. Take life easy; eat, drink and be merry." But we saw that God said to him, "You fool! This very night your life will be demanded from you."

It was the rich fool who said the "Eat, drink and be merry" part. But he said nothing at all about dying. God was the one to mention death, and it was a condemnation of the rich fool's attitude.

Eight Days a Week

You remember the old Beatles tune? It's a great song in which a guy tells his girl he needs her love "eight days a week." We know there are only seven days in a week, but the singer is saying he can't settle for that from his girl. He wants more, even if it's not possible. Seven days' worth of love isn't enough.

But in a different way, we want the week to have eight days, too. We even have a name for that eighth day. Maybe you know it? It's *Someday.* Other people know it as *Whenday,* but they're really the same day.

You say you haven't heard of *Someday* and *Whenday*? That's funny, because you use them all the time:

"Someday I'm going to go back and get my college degree."
"Someday I'm going to write a book."
"Someday I'm going to find a nice girl and settle down."
"Someday I'm going to tell my father I forgive him."

Or the other one:

"The day when I'm through sowing my wild oats, I'll date a woman I can respect."
"The day when I finally get a good job, I'll be able to get serious about marriage."
"The day when we get a new home, we can have kids."
"The day when we pay off our mortgage, we can take a family vacation."
"The day when the kids leave home, we can plan for retirement."
"The day when we finally retire, we can enjoy life."
"The day when we're too old to enjoy life, we'll think about God."

Someday/Whenday. The eighth days in the week.

Oh, you won't find them on any calendar. Because Someday and Whenday never happen. There's always another day between Today and Someday. There's always another Whenday to postpone the last one to. We can "Someday" and "Whenday" from week to week to month to month to year to year to decade to decade until all the Somedays and all the Whendays add up to Never. We're so good at that.

But the rich guy in this story thought his Someday had come. He had put everything off to that day. Oh, he was ready for it. Oooh, he could taste it. He had always said Someday he was going to eat, drink, and be merry, and Someday was here!

And then God said, "You fool. I didn't make you to live for

Someday. I didn't make you to put off the true responsibilities and joys of life for the Whenday you wanted. I made you to *live now,* not later. You have wasted everything pursuing your plans and your wishes and your Somedays without giving one thought to the Today I gave you. And now your Someday is Never."

As I said before, Ouch.

Here's what the Bible says about living now: "Redeem . . . the time, because the days are evil" (Eph. 5:16 NKJV). I like the way one modern translation puts it: "These are evil times, so make every minute count" (CEV).

We say that last part so many times, it's become a cliché. We no longer listen to it. We just say, "Oh, yes, make every minute count, of course!" and go on wasting our lives with Somedays and Whendays, never realizing that the minutes we are supposed to make count are the very ones we are living right at this moment.

It's time to change that. It's time to abandon the Somedays and Whendays and start living Todays. I have a favorite verse I say in the morning. It's the ultimate statement of living now: "This is the day the Lord has made; [I] will rejoice and be glad in it!" (Ps. 118:24 KJV).

So many people get caught looking back at their pasts, emphasizing something that has come and gone. Something somebody said to them or they said to somebody. Something somebody did to them or they did to somebody. And they make that something and that somebody so big they blot out God, and a day long, long past becomes the only day of their lives.

Other people get caught looking forward, anticipating that big Someday when everything will magically fall into place and become absolutely perfect, as if God could only make one perfect day, ever. But that perfect day is never today. Oh, no, something is always not quite right about today. Something is not quite finished, something is not quite put into place. But tomorrow—that has to be better. Maybe. But more likely it will be the same, because, you know, Someday takes time. Today is just way too soon, and not nearly as good as Someday will be. If it comes.

It's time to stop living for Someday and Whenday. It's time to live *now.*

In his book *Today Matters,* John Maxwell quotes the following:

> **The Lifebuilder's Creed**
> BY DALE WITHERINGTON
>
> Today is the most important day of my life.
> Yesterday with its successes and victories, struggles and failures is gone forever.
> The past is past.
> Done.
> Finished.
> I cannot relive it. I cannot go back and change it.
> But I will learn from it and improve my TODAY.
>
> TODAY. This moment. NOW.
> It is God's gift to me and it is all that I have.
>
> Tomorrow with all its joys and sorrows, triumphs and troubles isn't here yet.
> Indeed, tomorrow may never come.
> Therefore, I will not worry about tomorrow.
>
> Today is what God has entrusted to me.
> It is all that I have. I will do my best in it.
> I will demonstrate the best of me in it—
> my character, giftedness, and abilities—
> to my family and friends, clients and associates.
> I will identify those things that are most important to do TODAY,
> and those things I will do until they are done.
> And when this day is done
> I will look back with satisfaction at that
> which I have accomplished.

Then, and only then, will I plan my tomorrow,
Looking to improve upon Today, with God's help.

Then I shall go to sleep in peace . . . content.[1]

What if the rich man had lived that way? What if you did? How would it affect your life now? What kind of practice do you think it would be for eternity?

Not a bad start, I think.

So how do we live that way?

We learn how to be tuned in.

We learn how to enjoy the journey, not just the destination.

We learn how to "Just do it."

Be Tuned In

Several years ago our family went on a vacation to Lake George. We were having dinner by the lake. Lisa and the kids were laughing, but I wasn't. I was sitting at the table with them, but I was staring out over the lake. Lisa looked at me and said, "Are you with us?"

I didn't like that at all, and it wound up turning into an argument. After the kids had gone to bed, I brought up the moment. "I don't know why you're badgering me about whether or not I'm 'with you,'" I said to Lisa. "I'm here. I'm on vacation with you and the kids. We're having a good time."

Lisa replied, "A lot of the times when you're with us, you're really not there. When you're here, you don't focus. You're not engaged with us. You're here, but you're not."

Of course, I didn't get it. Clueless male that I am, I had to defend myself to the hilt. But when I was alone with God later that evening, he wasn't about to let me off. "She's right," he pointed out. "You're not there. You need to disengage from the stuff that doesn't matter and focus on the stuff that does."

If you're a guy reading this, you might be twitching a little in your seat. And if you're a woman reading this, you're highlighting the passage for some man in your life to read. (Sorry about that, guys.)

I'll use an analogy that every guy will love: jet fighter pilots. Oh, yeah. Now that is man stuff, right there. Screaming speeds, roaring engines, swooping moves, blazing guns, *ZZZOOOOMMM!* Put me in the cockpit, right, guys? We're made for it.

Except we're not.

One of the first things that potential fighter pilots have to be taught is a little trick called "situational awareness." A pilot has to learn how to see all around him—to see from the corners of his eyes. He has to learn to be aware of what's in the sky with him, not just in front of the jet, but also to the side, the rear, above, below—the full 360-degree sphere around him, from horizon to horizon, from ground to space. In fighter-pilot parlance, a pilot who loses his situational awareness is soon to lose his life. You can't daydream in the cockpit. You can't think about the game tomorrow, what the boss said yesterday, or how you're going to fit in time to do the taxes. You have to be right there, in that moment, completely in tune with your aircraft and with what is happening around you. If you aren't, you're dead.

Some would-be pilots never master it. They don't know how to be "tuned in" in their planes. That failure is dangerous to them and their wingmen. They don't cut it.

Guys (and ladies), if you're going to cut it as a Live Now person, you have to be tuned in.

When you're with your family, be tuned in.

When you're with your spouse, be tuned in.

When you're with your kids, be tuned in.

When you're with a close friend, be tuned in.

Don't let what you need to do, or what you've already done, or what may or may not happen rob you from living in the moment.

I'm not saying this is easy. I'm the type of person who is always thinking about the next goal, the next achievement, or the next project. Sometimes, because I'm so focused on the next thing, I don't truly engage in the moment—and my wife is quick to let me know about it. So I'm writing to myself as much as to you.

That doesn't mean I don't have goals, any more than it means a pilot doesn't have a destination. I'm not suggesting we all phase out and "just be, man." I'm saying just the opposite. I'm saying we need to be fully aware, crystal clear, and committed to the day—*this* day. Now. All in, all there, tuned in and ready to go.

That's the first step in living now.

Enjoy the Journey, Not Just the Destination

I know that's a cliché, but one of the reasons clichés stick around is because there's truth in them. For example, I love vacations with my family (on which, by the way, my wife now tells me that I have greatly improved at being tuned in). My favorite family-vacation spot is Disney World. My family and I go at least once a year.

On our first trip, we stayed in a hotel off the Disney property. We went to the parks without really planning anything. We ate whenever we wanted to eat, mostly going to restaurants in Orlando, choosing whatever we felt like at the time.

But the second year we decided to go for the whole Disney experience. Not only did we decide to stay in a Disney hotel, we decided to use the Disney meal plan. When you use the Disney meal plan, you have to make reservations at every restaurant where you want to eat. If you didn't make a reservation, you couldn't go to the restaurant you wanted. Since we were going "full Disney," we wanted to make sure the kids got to eat breakfast with Mickey and Minnie and dinner with Cinderella and Pluto.

Lisa always handles the planning for these trips. So before we even left she asked me things like "What time do you want to eat breakfast on Saturday morning?" And I'm thinking, *Saturday? Today is Tuesday. How the heck do I know what time I want to eat on Saturday?* But I'd throw out a time, and she'd look at the computer and say, "They don't have an eight-thirty time, we have to take seven." *Seven o'clock? As in "A.M."?* As in "get up really early"? On vacation?

But it was that way with every reservation. They never had the time we really wanted, or if they had the time, it wasn't on the day we wanted, so we'd have to plan a different day.

As you've probably realized, when I'm on vacation I don't like to be "on the clock." I like to get up whenever I want to get up and eat whenever I want to eat. But on this trip we couldn't do that. Every night we had to plan how soon we'd have to get everybody up and dressed so we could make our breakfast reservations. And if we were in the parks all day, we had to keep a close eye on our watches, especially if our dinner reservation was in Epcot while we were in the Magic Kingdom, because it can take an hour just to get from one park to another if the monorail and bus lines are long. As a result, our entire vacation became about rushing to whatever reservation we had. The fun, relaxing time we expected became a hectic race to be somewhere else rather than enjoying where we were.

Sometimes in life we get caught up in the same way. We focus so much on destinations that we forget that the journey is part of things as well—sometimes the most important part. But we become stuck in a "get there" mentality, treating life as if it's all rush hour on a crowded highway. *I want to get there! Get out of my way! Don't point out the signs or the scenery or the other people on the road. No, I don't want to pull off at the overlook. No, I don't want to look at the sunset. No, I don't care about the stars in the sky or how the moon looks on the river. Yes, that little roadside stand probably does have good peaches, but I want to get there! Where is there? I don't know, it's my destination! What's my destination?*

Well, when I'm a kid, my destination is to be sixteen, so I can drive.

When I'm sixteen, my destination is to be eighteen, so I can drive away from my parents.

When I'm eighteen my destination is to be twenty-one, so I can really drive away from my parents.

When I'm twenty-one, my destination is to graduate from college so I can drive back home to my parents.

When I graduate, my destination is to get that great job so I can move away from my parents into my own apartment.

When I get that job, my destination is to get that promotion so I can move away from that apartment and into a fancy house.

When I get that promotion, my destination is to retire so I can move a thousand miles away from that fancy house.

Funny how the destination keeps moving, and no matter how much I race I never quite catch up with it. How about you?

We need to stop chasing destinations and start appreciating the journey. We need to pull off at the overlooks and consider life. We need to notice the people around us and the blessings of each moment. We need to see the sunset, the moonrise over the water, the stars in the night sky. We need to stop and eat fresh peaches at the side of the road. Yes, we do have a final destination ahead, but if the destination were all there was to it, God wouldn't have bothered to give us life here. The destination creates the journey, and the journey leads to the destination. God created both of them, and both are meant to be treasured.

Just Do It

Yep. I stole that line from Nike. But you know what? Nike stole it from God, so I think I'm okay borrowing it back.

Oh, you didn't know Nike got that from God? Well, what exactly does Nike mean with that slogan "Just Do It"? Don't they mean "No more excuses. No more putting it off. No more being afraid. Lace up your sneakers (preferably ours) and *go*"? That's pretty much the point, isn't it?

Now have a look at what Jesus said to some people who were quibbling with him about their purpose in life:

> On the road someone asked if he could go along. "I'll go with you, wherever," he said.
>
> Jesus was curt: "Are you ready to rough it? We're not staying in the best inns, you know."
>
> Jesus said to another, "Follow me."
>
> He said, "Certainly, but first excuse me for a couple of days, please. I have to make arrangements for my father's funeral."
>
> Jesus refused. "First things first. Your business is life, not death. And life is urgent: Announce God's kingdom!"
>
> Then another said, "I'm ready to follow you, Master, but first excuse me while I get things straightened out at home."
>
> Jesus said, "No procrastination. No backward looks. You can't put God's kingdom off till tomorrow. Seize the day." (Luke 9:58–62 *The Message*)

Jesus was saying to those men, "You know what to do. So just do it." He was saying, "Don't give me empty promises or lame excuses. Don't say you're going to do something you know you won't do, and don't say you're going to do something and then come up with reasons not to do it. That won't wash with me. No more excuses. No more putting it off. No being afraid. Just do it."

So, yes, I'm claiming "Just do it" back for God.

If you have something you know you're supposed to do, just do it.

If there's someone you know needs help and you can help them, just do it.

If there's a change you need to make in your life, just do it.

Maybe you know you need to find a church and learn more about God. Well, then, go find one.

Maybe you know you need to pray more. Well, then, pray.

Maybe you know you need to give more. Well, then, give.

Maybe you know you need to be more involved in the church you're in. Well, then, get more involved.

Maybe you know you need to find a job that honors God and the purpose he made you for. Well, then, go find that job.

Maybe you know you need to start working on your marriage. Well, then, work on it.

No more excuses. No more empty, insincere promises. No more putting it off. No more being afraid. Lace up your life sneakers and *go.* Just do it!

Be tuned in.

Enjoy the journey, not just the destination.

Just do it.

Live *now.*

CHAPTER 29

Live Legacy

SOMETIME TOWARD THE end of the Clinton presidency the word *legacy* began to pop up all over the media. It's an old word, but for some reason it became the buzzword of the day among politicians and pundits, and it just seems to hang around. "What will be his legacy?" some reporter will say when talking about a soon-to-retire official. And they don't just say it about politicians. Nowadays athletes have legacies. Movie stars have legacies. It's gotten more than a little bizarre.

But what's really amusing is that what all these people pronounce as being some celebrity's "legacy"—what they are remembered for—quite often isn't what they are remembered for at all. A president who expected to be remembered for great statesmanship instead is remembered for scandal. An athlete who expected to be remembered for incredible feats on the playing field is instead remembered for using steroids. It can go the other way as well: a nobody on a train platform suddenly is remembered for leaping on the tracks to save someone's life. Legacies are tricky things to predict. Most times people's legacies don't become clear until they're gone.

Take a look at this list:

Mark Twain . . . . writing *The Adventures of Tom Sawyer* and *Huckleberry Finn*
Alexander Graham Bell. . . . inventing the telephone
Mother Teresa . . . . caring for the poor

Billy Graham . . . . preaching the gospel
Vince Lombardi . . . . coaching football
Babe Ruth. . . . . hitting home runs
Eddie Taylor. . . . . (Eddie who? Read on.)

Some people make indelible impressions on the world. Others, not so much. But the truth is, even if we won't be remembered for something as big as inventing the telephone, we will be remembered. And deep down we all want to be remembered for something significant. We all want our lives to matter. We all want to be remembered for the right things.

Remember that last name on our list—Eddie Taylor? I knew him just as a regular guy. He and his wife were members of our church for twenty years, always there, always serving. Eddie's big thing was cooking. His specialty was barbecued ribs. He was famous for them. He'd give them away to people just so he could cook more of them. Whenever the church had a barbecue, Eddie was always there with his ribs. That's how I knew Eddie: this good joe who loved to cook. And I thought that would be his legacy.

Eddie was still a young man when he passed away; he had struggled with liver disease for years, and it just finally caught up with him. He and his wife, Chrissy, had no children, so I was prepared for a small funeral. But when the day came, a large group of young adults arrived at the funeral, and Chrissy introduced them as "their children." A more diverse group of children you couldn't imagine. There were clearly no DNA matches here.

But as the story came out, we all learned who Eddie really was. These young adults were Eddie and Chrissy's foster children. You couldn't count the number who came up to say words about Eddie, and every single one described him as "the dad I had never had."

One particular young lady touched my heart. She had Down syndrome. Her words were simple but eloquent. She told how until the time she lived with Eddie and Chrissy, she had had a sad life. She had never heard the words "I love you" or "You're beautiful."

But she heard them from Eddie and Chrissy. In the two of them she found a father and mother who treated her like a true daughter. Under their love she came to see herself as beautiful, when before she had always thought she was ugly. And she allowed her beauty to be noticed by a young man, a friend who joined the family for a trip to the amusement park and eventually became her husband.

She told how the day of her wedding, Eddie walked her down the aisle, his face as proud as if she had been his own. Eddie's love had made it possible for her to love herself, and to love her husband. "I would not be here today," she said, "if it were not for Eddie being the dad I never had."

That was the legacy that Eddie lived. Not ribs. Not being a regular guy. Not helping out at the church. No, Eddie's legacy was the greatest legacy of all—love.

Eddie knew the truth about legacies that all the politicians and personalities and pundits miss. Legacies aren't something you leave; they're something you live.

And the way you live a legacy is to live people.

CHAPTER 30

Live People

IF WE WANT to prepare for eternity, we should do everything in our power to make other people the central focus of our lives. After all, aren't people the most important thing to God? People are why God made the world. People are why God made heaven. People are why God gave his Son, Jesus, to die on the cross. God revolves his whole existence around people. If God's life revolves around people, shouldn't our lives revolve around people, too? They're the whole point of eternity!

Now I know some of you are thinking, *I'm just not a people person, Frank. What are you expecting me to do? What does "live people" even mean?* Relax. To live people, you have to follow only three simple guidelines:

Love people.
Reconcile with people.
Forgive people.

That's all it takes.

Love People

A few years ago a man started coming to our church, and I could tell from the moment I met him that he was really in love with God. He loved to talk about God and all the great things God was doing in his life. Even when the economy turned south and he went through some financially trying times, he always remained positive about what God was going to do. You would never hear him say anything negative or harsh. He had a wonderful marriage and a beautiful daughter, and I assumed that what I saw was what he had always been: an upbeat, loving man of faith.

He started offering to help me out whenever I traveled by driving me to the airport and back. Naturally, during these private drives together, I got to know him very well. And over time I learned his real story. Many years before he came to our church, he had been married to another woman. He admitted to being a terrible husband. At that time he had a horrible temper—he'd beat up anyone he thought even looked at him the wrong way. He loved to fight, and while he wasn't physically abusive, his wife was often caught in the whirlwind of his constant anger. Needless to say, that marriage soon fell apart.

As he dealt with the aftermath of that divorce, he finally began to examine who he was and why he behaved as he did. He explained to me that when he was a child, his mother had never once told him that she loved him. He didn't place the blame on her for his decisions, but he had to recognize the source of that anger in order to give it to God.

It took years, he said, for God to work that anger out of him. Today, whenever you hear him talk to his wife and daughter, you can hear the care he takes to say loving words to them. Because he never heard those words himself, he realizes their crucial power in the lives of others.

His story reminds us that to be loved is fundamental to human life. We *have* to have it. Without it we shrivel up. We coarsen, we collapse, we turn upon ourselves and gnaw at our own souls. We become cynical, selfish, even savage—all because we do not hear the words "I love you." And we don't hear them *because we don't say them*. We have to say them.

"Oh, the people I love know that I do. I don't have to get

mushy like that." Yes, you do. It's not enough to just hope they figure it out. Say the words, just as God does.

- "But God has shown us how much he loves us in that while we were yet sinners Christ died for us." (Rom. 5:8 NIV)
- "For God so loved the world that he gave his only begotten son, that whosoever would believe in him would not perish but have eternal life." (John 3:16 NIV)
- "'I have loved you with an everlasting love.'" (Jer. 31:3 NIV)

How's that for a valentine? Not only does God say he loves you, he says his love is everlasting. Eternal. Forever. Not just yesterday, when you sat in church and tried to smile at the sermon. Not just tomorrow, when you go out on a picnic on a gorgeous spring day. But yesterday, today, and tomorrow—all of them, from beginning to end, every moment, every second.

- when you shouted at your kids because you had a bad day at work, God loved you
- when you snuck a peek at that Web site with the tempting title, God loved you
- when you called that woman who cut you off in traffic a you-know-what, God loved you
- when you yelled at God because your wife is dying of breast cancer and leaving you and your four-year-old daughter behind, God loved you
- when you took your first breath, God loved you
- when you take your last breath, God will love you
- when you fear today, God loves you
- when you worry about tomorrow, God loves you
- when you enter eternity and on every day afterward, without end, God loves you

Make your "I love yous" like God's. Don't just assume you've "telegraphed" your love to those who matter to you. Say the words. Not just once, but over and over again. Make those words as everlasting as you can. Say them again and again and again. Say them until you die. And if you do, you can't help but fulfill the first guideline—you will love people.

Reconcile with People

Do you remember Fonzie from the seventies TV series *Happy Days*? Everything about him was cool. He rode a motorcycle, wore a black leather jacket, and if he snapped his fingers, every chick in the room would rush to hang on his arms. But there was one thing Fonzie couldn't do: he couldn't say the words "I was wrong." He'd try to form the phrase, but it would come out in unintelligible mush: "I was wuuuuurrrrrroooooouuuuuwwwooo." He couldn't admit his errors, and he couldn't apologize.

When Lisa and I first got married, I took very seriously the concept that I was spiritually responsible for the relationship. I believed that making sure things were right between us fell more on me than it did on her. I made up my mind that no matter what disagreement we might have, I would be the one to initiate reconciliation. I would not be "too cool" to apologize. In fact, whether I was right or wrong, I determined to keep the peace, and that I would always be the first to say "I'm sorry."

This worked well for about six months.

When you're newly married, the first few years you spend figuring each other out. And often that first year is the make-or-break year, when you either learn how to work things out or you don't. You're two different people, thrown into a confined space, and all the little idiosyncrasies that were so adorable when you were dating become like stinging gnats of annoyance.

We were no different, so naturally we had our share of newlywed arguments. But noble and holy young husband that I was, if we had an argument, I would close it by saying, "I'm sorry." That would end it, and we'd move along. But the thing was, at least 50 percent of the time Lisa would be the one who was wrong. (I'm saying that to sound fair, because naturally in my view it was more like 100 percent of the time. After all, I was the spiritual professional.) So a little bit of resentment began to build up inside me. I started to think, *Sheesh, why doesn't she admit she's wrong some of the time?*

Then one time we had a big disagreement, to put it mildly. In my mind she was clearly 1,000 percent wrong. By that time I had learned that one of my wife's weaknesses was being stubborn. She would absolutely refuse to say she was sorry. So I was thinking, *After all those times I said I was sorry, even though I knew I was right, here she is, regardless of whether she is right or wrong, and she won't say she's sorry. Well, I'm not going to say "I'm sorry" this time. It's her turn.*

Sure enough, we had a standoff—for three days. I wasn't going to apologize. She wasn't going to apologize. So we didn't talk to each other for three days. (I told you the woman was stubborn.)

Finally, I had to get before God—it's unavoidable in this business—and said, "God, about this woman you gave me . . ." I can sound just like Adam. "This woman is not going to say she's sorry. Evidently, one of her weaknesses is that she's a downright stubborn-as-a-mule woman. But you have given me the spiritual responsibility in this union, and I guess I'm just going to have to swallow my pride and say 'I'm sorry' anyway." (I told you I was the spiritual professional.)

So I felt better, apologized, and we reconciled for a while. But soon we were back at it. We finally agreed to have an "irritation" session, where we shared what annoyed us in the other person. She gave her list, and I gave mine. And the first thing I said was "What irritates me is that in the first six months of our marriage, you have never once initiated reconciliation. I always have, and I feel like you owe it to me." And later, after I apologized, we got that all worked out. I'm happy to say that she's not nearly as stubborn as she used to be, though she's still more stubborn than I am (that would be short-tempered, impatient, perfectionist, not-tuned-in me).

Even though the Fonz didn't see saying "I was wrong" as cool, our heavenly Father sees it as one of the godliest virtues we can demonstrate. Look at Christ. The Scripture says that Jesus came "to seek and to save that which was lost"(Luke 19:10 NKJV). He didn't wait for us to come to him, even though it was clearly our turn; he came to us. Paul puts it this way: "For God was in Christ, reconciling the world to himself, no longer counting people's sins against them. And he gave us this wonderful message of reconciliation" (2 Cor. 5:19 NLT).

Did you catch that last part? Jesus came to us—he was the one who initiated reconciliation, and so should we. Saying "I'm sorry" healed my marriage and helped me begin to build my life around the people who mattered most to me: my wife and kids. What if I had refused to say "I'm sorry"? What if I had acted like the Fonz? Maybe my marriage wouldn't be as strong as it is today. Maybe that three-day standoff would have turned into four and then five and then a week, a month, a year. Maybe my kids wouldn't have a mom and dad who were together. And maybe their lives would be drastically different, and so would mine. We should not overlook the power of saying the words "I'm sorry" and how it impacts not just our own lives, but also the lives of all the people around us.

Forgive People

When our kids were younger, Lisa and I taught them to be quick to apologize when they did something wrong. On the flip side, whenever somebody said to them "I'm sorry" or "Please forgive me," we taught them that their response should be "I forgive you." Of course, this was primarily to deal with all their brother-sister squabbles.

My son, Joseph, is very literal. If you tell Joseph to take two twelve-inch steps, he'll put a ruler on the floor to measure his steps. When he and his sister were little he was also usually the one to start a squabble. He's the younger, so he was always testing and teasing and bothering his sister. Nicole would get exasperated with him. But he was always quick to repent. He would go to her and say, "I'm sorry, Nicole." Most of the time, Nicole would respond, "I forgive you," as we had taught her. But sometimes she wouldn't. Sometimes she would just say, "Okay."

That wasn't enough for Joseph. He would then burst into almost a tantrum. "You didn't say you forgive me! You need to say you forgive me! Mommy, Daddy, she didn't say she'd forgive me!"

Even if I was disciplining Joseph for something he had done wrong and he said he was sorry, if I didn't immediately say I forgave him he would start to cry. Forgiveness was very important to him.

It is just as important to all of us, even if we don't want to admit it. And that importance goes both ways: forgiveness affects the forgiver as much as the one forgiven. We know, for instance, that harboring bitterness and chronic anger can be detrimental to physical health. The refusal to forgive, the desire to hold a grudge, or the urge to wish hurt on another can have physiological effects ranging from chronic pain to high blood pressure. An unforgiving spirit can corrode your physical health just as cigarette smoking, obesity, or a high-fat diet do.[1]

Forgiveness is also an important element in our mental and emotional health. When we refuse to forgive, we place emphasis on a particular event (or even a series of events) that locks us into that past moment. The event can be gone for good, but we trap our minds and thoughts there. Our fixation begins to color how we think of others, ourselves, our world, and even God. You can't really see what the world is like or what you are like because you're trapped in that unforgiven past. Remember that one of the things we should do is "live now." How can you live now if you're stuck reliving your past?

Forgiveness resolves that past. It breaks it off and lets it fall away. It frees both the forgiver and the forgiven.

But most of all, forgiveness allows us to be forgiven ourselves. Jesus said, "For if you forgive other people when they sin against you, your heavenly Father will also forgive you. But if you do not forgive others their sins, your Father will not forgive your sins" (Matt. 6:14–15 NIV). I like the way *The Message* puts it: "In prayer there is a connection between what God does and what you do. You can't get forgiveness from God, for instance, without also forgiving others. If you refuse to do your part, you cut yourself off from God's part."

Hard Can Be Simple

I know that saying the words "I forgive you" is not as easy as it sounds. It hurts to be wronged. When we hurt, our natural inclination is to strike back. And if that hurt is repeated or seemingly irreparable, our natural inclination is to hate. We want to get even. We want to pay back. We want to lash out. We want to have the last word. But that won't work. It won't change the hurt we've been done; it just means we wind up living in that hurt, feeding it, and making it grow. That doesn't do us any good at all.

So how do we break through that and say "I forgive you"?

We do it by trying to understand the why.

You've probably heard the phrase "Father, forgive them, for they do not know what they are doing." Jesus said it while hanging on the cross. But you may never have put that phrase in context of what was going on at the time. In the previous twenty-four hours, Jesus had been betrayed, arrested, abandoned, falsely accused, illegally tried, mocked, beaten, and whipped until his back ran with blood. He'd had a wreath of two-inch thorns jammed into his scalp. He'd been forced to carry a heavy beam of wood through the rough stone streets of Jerusalem. He'd had iron spikes driven into his hands and feet. He was almost entirely naked, hanging in front of a crowd who reviled him with abuse. He was in excruciating pain. Every breath came out of agony as he forced his body to rise to let air into his lungs just to survive only a little longer. And yet he used that breath to speak. Did he curse his torturers? Did he mock his mockers? Did he cry out, "You're going to pay for this! You're all going to hell!"? No. He said, "Father, forgive them, for they do not know what they are doing" (Luke 23:34 NIV).

Jesus saw beyond his own pain. He saw beyond the surface of the faces jeering at him. He saw right into the hearts of the soldiers and the rulers and the religious leaders, and saw their complete lack of understanding. In the midst of his betrayal, in the midst of injustice, in the midst of unimaginable agony, Jesus found empathy for his tormentors. And he used that empathy to forgive.

Can you find empathy, too? I know it's tough. I know it doesn't take the pain away. That's God's job. But fortunately we can ask God to help us understand the other person's why. For example:

> Maybe he's been hurt so much he knows no other way to act.
> Maybe she's been abused and knows no other life.
> Maybe his trust has been violated and he cannot trust again.
> Maybe her father cheated on her mother, and she suspects all men of being like Dad.
> Maybe his boss ridicules him every day, making him feel like less of a man.
> Maybe his friend stabbed him in the back, making him suspicious of your promises.
> Maybe her teacher made her feel stupid, and she has to feel smarter than someone else.

We can't know all the maybe's, but with God's help, we can try. And if we can find a way to empathize, God can help us say the words "I forgive you." And like loving people and reconciling with people, forgiving people impacts the lives of those around us for all of eternity.

Kerry and Chris Shook have a ministry based on their book *One Month to Live: Thirty Days to a No-Regrets Life,* which puts forth an interesting challenge: for the next month, act as if you had only those thirty days left on earth. What would you do?

On their Web site, the Shooks share the story of TerriLynn McDonough, who took the challenge to heart. TerriLynn's son had been murdered at college. The murderer had been caught and convicted, and TerriLynn was invited to speak at his sentencing. This is what Terry said to her son's murderer: "If I had one month to live, I'd want to forgive everyone, including you. I choose to forgive you for my own sake, because I see Jesus standing next to you, with his hand on your shoulder, begging me to forgive you. And if you somehow become a saver of lives instead of a destroyer of lives, then maybe my son's death won't have been in vain."[2]

For the rest of her challenge, TerriLynn wrote letters to the young man in prison. She lived up to her words of forgiveness, and the young man responded. In that time he became a Christian and was baptized in prison.

Shook asked TerriLynn how she was able to forgive her son's murderer. She replied, "I just stepped up and God gave me the power. I didn't think I could."[3]

God gave her the power, and God can give it to you as well. If God can give a mother the power to forgive her son's murderer, is there really anything God can't give you the power to forgive? Is your hurt really beyond God—the God who made the universe, the God who made you? Of course it isn't. If you will let God give you the power to forgive, he will. And in freeing others, you will suddenly find yourself free.

That's the power of forgiving people: it impacts people for all eternity.

Why Are People So Important?

If you're still wondering why people are important, I want you to consider the following question: What are the only things that we know without a doubt will be in heaven?

The answer is God and people. The Bible makes that abundantly clear. Even if we don't know what all the imagery and metaphors for heaven mean, we know this truth: God wants people to be in heaven, and he's moved heaven and earth to make that happen. Everything else, the Bible says, is passing away—but not people. So if we're going to build our lives on what eternally matters, that's where our lives should be built: on God and on people.

The apostle John made that point clear in his first letter to the Christian community. John is often called the "disciple of love," and his message revolves around it:

> Dear friends, since God so loved us, we also ought to love one another. No one has ever seen God; but if we love one another, God lives in us and his love is made complete in us. . . .
>
> We love because he first loved us. Whoever claims to love God yet hates a brother or sister is a liar. For whoever does not love their brother and sister, whom they have seen, cannot love God, whom they have not seen. And he has given us this command: Anyone who loves God must also love their brother and sister. (1 John 4:11–12, 19–21 NIV)

If you want to live for God, it's obvious—you have to live people.

CHAPTER 31

Live Loved

MY LAST POINT may be the most crucial of all, and the one we humans mess up the most. You may remember a few years ago when the concept of self-esteem became all the rage. We were told that part of the problem with society was that our kids didn't have enough self-esteem, and that if we all just made them feel better about themselves, everything would be perfect.

Well, I'm not going to say that feeling good about yourself doesn't have value, but we have some odd ways of finding a basis for it. In this world we get all sorts of messages about our self-esteem, and most of them don't make things better at all. We've gotten self-esteem confused with pride—and by *pride* I don't mean "confidence," I mean the mistaken notion that feeling good about ourselves comes only by being better than someone else, or denying that there might be anything wrong with us. The first makes you either a snob or a bully; the latter makes you delusional. Neither is a true source of self-worth.

Let's go back to that story of our rich fool. He was clearly full of self-esteem. You can't find a more confident revelation of self-esteem than all his "I wills." "I will tear down my old barns and build new, bigger ones." "I will take it easy; eat, drink and be merry." He sounds like a real go-getter and a man of success, and a fun party guy, too. Donald Trump and P. Diddy rolled into one.

But what gave him all that confidence? Didn't his sense of self-worth come entirely from his wealth? He's not eating, drinking, and being merry because he has good friends to do it with. He's not celebrating because God has been good to him. He's all about the Benjamins. He's got money, and because he's got money, he thinks he matters. And as we see at the end of the story, the Benjamins are worthless.

Before you judge the rich fool, ask yourself if you're any different. His source of self-worth was his money, but what is it for you? A house instead of an apartment? A bigger house instead of the one you're in now? A luxury car? A corner office? A more important-sounding job title? A flashier career? Less weight? More muscle? Nicer clothes, better teeth, a new hairdo—maybe a better-looking spouse?

Ouch.

We're all the same as the rich fool, striving to find our self-worth in things that cannot give it to us. And in today's economy we've had a rude awakening to just how flawed those sources of self-worth are. When the stock market crashes and the housing market takes a dive and you find yourself up to your ears in a mortgage you can't pay because you just lost that flashy job with the fancy title, the self-worth you've built on those things crumbles into nothing.

The Billionaire Junkie

On April 5, 1976, a man lay dying. Though only seventy years old, he had the emaciated body of a man in his late nineties. His scraggly gray hair sprawled across his pillow; had he been able to stand, it would have hung down to his back. His fingernails and toenails were over an inch long, twisting grotesquely and covered in fungus. His skin hung loose, pale, and dry on his skeletal frame, and bedsores covered his back, arms, and legs. In places they were so deep they exposed bone. Needle scars from near-constant drug abuse marked his inner thighs. Internally, his kidneys and digestive organs were shutting down due to years of malnutrition and neglect.

But he wasn't some third-world poverty case in a hut, or a homeless addict lying in a filthy alley. He was lying in a custom Lear jet, flying from the Mexican resort city of Acapulco to Houston, Texas, surrounded by "aides" and his personal physician (all highly paid to supply him with drugs and obey whatever crazed whim entered his mind). He owned homes and hotels throughout California, the Bahamas, and Las Vegas. His aerospace company had government contracts with the military and NASA. His estimated wealth at the time was in the billions, making him one of the wealthiest men in the world.

His name was Howard Hughes—billionaire, record-setting pilot, instinctive inventor—and he died a junkie.[1] All his wealth, fame, and accomplishments couldn't give his life the meaning he truly desired. His self-worth was built on worthless things, and he died never knowing what his worth really was.

Realize Your Worth

There is only one way to realize how valuable you are. It doesn't come from what you own, what you do, who you know, or who you are. In fact, your real worth doesn't come from you at all.

Your real worth comes from God.

You are worth exactly what he says you're worth, no more and no less.

But the good news is, he says you're worth everything. Not just some things. Not just bling and Benjamins or titles and awards, but life and death themselves. He says you're worth eternity.

Because he loves you. And he wants you to know that, every moment, every day.

That's a love you can live in.

You can't add to it by purchasing anything.

You can't take away from it by losing anything.

You can't do anything to prove it, or make it more.

You can't do anything to lose it, or make it less.

The stock market can't take it away from you.
The bank can't foreclose on it.
The boss can't fire you from it.
The kids can't tease you because you don't have it.
It's there. It's yours. All you have to do is live in it.
All you have to do is live loved.

How do you know God loves you? The next chapter has the answer, and it's summed up in one name.

Jesus.

PART VII

Jesus: Is He the Only Way?

CHAPTER 32

The Ultimatum That Isn't

There comes a time in every parent's life where we find ourselves saying the one thing we swore we'd never say; the one thing our own parents said that just made us stew: "Because I said so." It was a lousy answer when we were kids, and we knew it. It's still a lousy answer when we're adults. But there are moments when we say it anyway. Maybe because there really isn't time to explain all the ramifications of what will happen if Junior doesn't drink his milk and eat his vegetables, or because that explanation is beyond Junior's grasp, or even because we're not quite sure how to explain it anyway. So we hand down the ultimatum. We hate it and Junior hates it and we wonder why we did that.

Nobody likes an ultimatum. We hear an ultimatum, and we get into fighting mode. We just boil. We don't like people telling us what to do.

Hey, the nation I call home came about because the Founding Fathers got fed up with somebody else telling them what to do. They heard an ultimatum and reached for the muskets.

So it's no wonder that some people hear "Jesus is the only way" and go into full minuteman mode.

"How dare you say that?"

"Where do you get off telling me what I have to believe?"

"How can you claim that your religion is right and everybody else's is wrong?"

And I can't say I blame people for those reactions. It's a pretty bold claim to make. It's in your face. And it sounds like the ultimatum of ultimatums—not "Believe it or not" but "Believe it or else."

Hey, I don't like being told what I have to do any more than the next guy. Just ask my wife.

But do you know when an ultimatum isn't an ultimatum? When it's simply the truth.

For example, I recently took my car in to be serviced. The mechanic told me I needed new brake pads. He showed me the worn-out ones on my car and handed me the estimate. I looked at the price and said, "Whoa. Are you sure I need new pads?"

"Yep. Without them your car won't be safe to drive."

"You must be mistaken about that. How can you say my car won't be safe to drive? I'll just drive slower; then it will be safe."

The mechanic shook his head. "Driving slower won't do it. You've got to have brakes to stop."

"No I don't! What about those parachute things I see on drag racers? I can get one of those."

The mechanic looked at me a little oddly. "That really won't work, Mr. Santora. All you need is some good brake pads."

"It's *Pastor* Santora, thank you very much, and I'll decide what I need. Hey—I know! I saw pictures of some wagons from the 1800s, and they all had this stick bolted on the side that they just jammed against the wheel. I could do that."

"Uhh . . ."

"Or I could just do like my son does when he wants to stop his bike and drag my feet on the ground. I saw Superman do that in a movie once."

"You're a funny guy, Pastor, I can see that. But why don't we just put on some new brake pads?"

"Stop telling me I have to have new brake pads! You don't know that's the only solution. You're just trying to make a sale. There could be hundreds of ways of stopping my car that you haven't told me or don't even know about!"

The mechanic nodded. "Okay, I confess. I do know one way you can stop your car without brake pads."

"Aha! I knew it. What's that?"

He slapped the keys into my hand. "You can go drive it into a lake."

Okay, yes, I made that conversation up. But why don't we argue like that with the mechanic when he tells us we have to have new brakes? Why don't we argue like that with the dentist when he tells us that our tooth hurts because we have a cavity and he has to fill it? Why don't we argue like that with our doctor when she tells us we have a broken arm and it has to be put in a cast? Because we know they aren't issuing ultimatums at all. They're just telling us the truth.

The question, then, isn't whether the statement "Jesus is the only way" is an ultimatum or not. The question is whether it's the truth.

CHAPTER 33

Can All Paths Really Lead to God?

THE BIGGEST ARGUMENT I hear against the claims of Christianity falls into the "nonexclusivity" category. Most of the time this is stated as "There are many paths to God. No one of them is any better than any of the others. All are equally valid."

At the risk of offending someone, I have to say that's utter nonsense.

First of all, if it were true, then *any* religion would need to be considered a "valid" path to God. Like, say, the ancient Aztec religion that practiced regular and bloody human sacrifices. Or the druids of ancient Britain, who strangled human sacrifices in the marshes or burned people in giant wicker idols. Or how about that cult in California back in the nineties whose members all committed ritual suicide in order to get to their paradise? Are we going to claim that these faiths were valid paths to God? There is a faith right now that says an undiscovered planet named Nibiru is going to slam into earth in December 2012, destroying everything. I have a hard time seeing how anyone could logically argue that any of these faiths represent a valid path to God.

But let's suppose we just restrict the claim to the "mainstream" faiths—Judaism, Buddhism, Islam, Daoism, Hinduism, Christianity, et cetera—the ones followed by millions or even billions of people. Can we say that these are all equally valid paths to God, and that it's wrong for a faith to claim an exclusive hold on the truth?

First of all, let's take that concept of "nonexclusive faiths," or the idea that all faiths are equally valid. The problem with that concept is that it contradicts itself. In order for the "nonexclusive faith" argument to be true, then any faith that is exclusive must be false. But if you exclude a faith for being exclusive, you are being exclusive yourself. You are saying "all are valid paths to God *except that one,*" and your whole premise collapses on itself.

Paradoxical Paths

The problem with the "many paths" argument is that it holds up only when the other paths *aren't* inherently exclusive. But they are. Each faith makes specific claims about who God is and how people should connect with him that exclude the claims of the other faiths.

Atheism holds that there is no God, or gods, of any kind, nor an afterlife, and you can't and shouldn't try to connect at all.

Judaism holds that there is one God only, and that you connect with him and the afterlife by following the teachings of the Torah and performing good works.

Islam holds that there is one God only, and that you connect with him and earn the afterlife by following the teachings of the Koran and strict adherence to its rules.

Buddhism does not argue for or against God, and says that you earn the afterlife (called Nirvana) by following the Eightfold Path and ridding yourself of desire.

Hinduism teaches that there is not one God, but many gods, and you earn reincarnation rather than an afterlife, and your whole goal is not to come back as something nasty like a slug, but eventually to become a god yourself.

Christianity teaches that there is one God who is also triune—the Father, the Son (Jesus), and the Holy Spirit—and that you connect with God through faith in Jesus Christ as his Son, and are given salvation into eternity through that faith and not your works.

I think you begin to see the problem here with the "many paths" argument. These six faiths are mutually exclusive in many ways. You cannot believe atheism and logically accept the other five in any way. You cannot believe strictly in Judaism and logically accept the other five as valid. You cannot believe in Islam and logically accept the other five as valid, and so on. And that's just six out of the many more faiths that exist, all claiming some exclusive truth that another faith itself excludes. So claiming that there are "many paths" is not a valid argument. It's really just an attempt to appear tolerant of the different religions in the world.

Tolerance isn't a bad thing, but it isn't a religious faith. It's a method of behavior, not a guide for belief. I can be tolerant of another person's faith without having to declare that faith as the truth. In fact, I can declare it not to be true at all and yet still be tolerant of its existence, just as I can be tolerant of fans of the Yankees, even though I know the best team in New York is the Mets. Tolerance is nothing to hang your faith hat on. (And it's faulty, too; if the Aztec religion of human sacrifice were still around, should we be tolerant of it?) On the surface, tolerance is a nice way to treat others, but you shouldn't base your eternity on it. You should base your eternity on the truth.

What Is Truth?

Early on in this book we examined the relationship between faith and evidence. As we said, faith is not and should not be blind. Faith is based on evidence. Faith is an act of intellect as well as an act of choice. I do not believe what I believe blindly or even out of wishful thinking, as some might claim, but because I have examined the evidence and I hold it to be truthful.

Already we have seen how this evidence points to the existence of an afterlife. Already we have seen how this evidence points to the existence of a soul. Already we have seen how this evidence points to the existence of God. Already we have seen how this evidence points to the existence of heaven, and yes, of hell. So now we have to ask ourselves, does this evidence point to a truth about faith?

CHAPTER 34

Profiling God

I LOVE COP SHOWS. *CSI, Law & Order, Numb3rs*—they're all great. For a while there was a show called *Profiler,* which featured a special agent in the FBI whose job was to "profile" criminals to aid the investigation in discovering who was responsible for a specific crime. The agent would examine the evidence from the crime scene, combined with the type of crime it was, the location, the victim, and so on to build a description of what the criminal was like: his motive, his job, his beliefs about the world, his social class, his economic class, his education level, et cetera. The profiler provided an amazingly elaborate picture of the person they should look for as a suspect.

Now that program might have been fiction, but it was based on real FBI procedures—the concept of examining clues to determine what type of person might have committed a specific crime so as to narrow down a potential pool of suspects. It's a technique that works well.

In fact, it's a technique that you and I use every day. Let's say you want to find a babysitter for your kids. Automatically, you have a list of characteristics that fit the sort of person you will trust alone with your children. I'm guessing it's a pretty specific list, and you're going to do your best to pick someone who fits the profile you've created. You're also going to judge potential babysitters with the clues they give you as to whether they're the sort of people you trust. If she shows up late, smelling of cigarette smoke, with tattoos and body piercings, and has some shady-looking guy sitting out in the car waiting on her, you're probably going to say, "No thank you," and close the front door. That may not be fair (there are plenty of perfectly nice people with at least some of those characteristics), but you've looked at the evidence and come to a conclusion about what type of person she is. And even if you admit that such a quick glance might be a shallow basis for assumption, you also understand that looking deeper is really just a case of examining more and better evidence to come to an understanding of who is standing at your door. You are creating a profile on which to base an important decision. It would be just as much of an error (if not more so) to accept anyone who walked in as to reject someone on just a bit of surface information.

Is your faith decision any less important? Of course not! It's the most important decision of your life, because it's not just about your life here on earth; it's about your eternity as well. Forever is a long time to regret a flippant decision.

So let's profile God. Let's see what God is like and what faith fits his profile.

What We Expect from God

The profile we're building isn't just a factor of what evidence tells us about God. There are clues based on what we ourselves expect of God. I don't mean how we define God, or what we wish God would do for us, as if he were the genie of Aladdin's lamp, ready to serve our every desire. Neither of those things would be God, and we know it. I'm talking about the things we find when we search deep down in our souls, when we consider what is good and right and true. When we do this, we begin to produce a deeper profile of God.

We need to be careful here; it's easy to go astray into what we want God to be like instead of what we know he must be like. But it's still a useful exercise.

We can break these expectations down into a few simple categories.

1. We Expect God to Demonstrate Miraculous Power

This fits with the evidence that we already have, that God is ultimately powerful. If any god can't perform miracles, he's not God. If he can, he's much closer to being the "real thing" than ones who can't. (It's important to note here that meeting just one point isn't sufficient to say, "That's God," not even miraculous power. That would be like saying, "I prefer a college-age babysitter" and hiring the next frat boy who showed up at the door. God has to be God on *all* fronts or he's something else entirely.)

2. We Expect God to Be Wise Above All Earthly Wisdom

God is ultimately intelligent, and since he is also eternal, he is also perfect in his knowledge. He knows the way the world is supposed to work. He knows the good choices from the bad, the right way from the wrong way, and he understands the complexities of human existence to the nth degree. So his wisdom is both original and elevated—unique in tone and profound in insight.

3. We Expect God to Be Morally Perfect

God is good and defines the meaning of goodness. As Socrates pointed out, a true god would be completely without sin; he would demonstrate no moral failing of any kind.

4. We Expect God to Be Understanding and Forgiving

God is perfect and good and possesses perfect knowledge. Therefore, he knows that we are not perfect. He knows our limitations as well as our abilities. Therefore, since mercy is a quality of being good, we would expect God to be merciful toward his far-from-perfect creations. We would expect him to be remarkably forgiving.

5. *We Expect God to Be Infinitely Loving*

God would know and understand love to its fullest expression. After all, he gave us the ability to love, the desire to be loved, and the ability to recognize love. Therefore, he would be able to love beyond all earthly forms of love. His love would be undeniable and ultimately astonishing.

6. *We Expect God to Be More Powerful Than Death*

Death is a quality of this universe. God created life and he created death. Therefore, he has ultimate power over both. God cannot die. He is eternal, without beginning or end.

That's a pretty tough act to stand up to. But it's our faith yardstick, if you will, and any god we look at should be measured against it.

Now you may suggest that I'm trying to set you up to say that Jesus fits all of the criteria I've just listed, and no one else does. Okay, yes, it's fair to say I believe Jesus does indeed fit the profile. But does that make the profile wrong? Look again at that list. Would you disagree that God should match any of the points on the list? I'm not asking whether you believe God or Jesus or anyone else matches the points—I'm asking whether ultimately they are indeed points you would expect of God in order for God to *be* God. Do each of these attributes fit the profile of God?

1. Supernaturally or miraculously powerful. Yes or no?
2. Ultimately wise. Yes or no?
3. Morally perfect. Yes or no?
4. Understanding and forgiving. Yes or no?
5. Infinitely loving. Yes or no?
6. More powerful than death. Yes or no?

This is not really a new standard, nor is it simply a Christian one. The philosopher Plato described how Socrates measured the ancient Greek gods according to a similar standard and found them wanting. Socrates pointed out that the Greeks believed in a standard of moral behavior that the gods established. Yet the stories told about those same gods revealed they did not hold to that standard. They exhibited petty jealousy, pursued adultery and even rape, inflicted capricious punishments, committed patricide and fratricide, and displayed every flawed human behavior from greed to drunkenness to lying. So either the standard was wrong, or the gods were not truly God at all. Socrates' gods didn't live up to the faith yardstick; they didn't fit the profile.

Does yours?

CHAPTER 35

The God Gauntlet, Part I

THERE'S NO SPACE here to put all faiths to the God test, and that's not my point. You can do that on your own, if you wish. Run Buddha, Confucius, Mohammed, Shiva, Zeus, the Goddess, and anyone else through that test and see what you discover. I think you'll run into a wall or two pretty quickly. My purpose is to run Jesus through that gauntlet and see what happens.

Jesus Takes the Test

1. Does Jesus Demonstrate Supernatural and Miraculous Ability?

Well, let's look at the record of Jesus' life, the four Gospels of Matthew, Mark, Luke, and John. Some people are going to reject these sources, saying the Gospels were written hundreds of years after Jesus' life, and that all the stories were made up. Except neither statement is true.

Let's take the account of Luke. Luke wrote two books of the Bible: the Gospel that bears his name, and the book of Acts, which follows the events in the lives of the twelve apostles after Jesus' death and reported resurrection. Acts also notably introduces us to the apostle Paul, the only apostle who was never a disciple of Christ during his ministry. Acts ends with Paul under house arrest in Rome, teaching Jewish and Gentile visitors about Jesus and waiting for his trial before the Caesar Nero.

This is an important point, because Acts does not cover that trial, or the four or five years after Paul had been set free before his rearrest and execution, along with Peter, in AD 67. Acts makes no mention of Peter's or Paul's death and doesn't even appear to anticipate either.

That's significant. Surely an account of the apostles written hundreds of years later would include the martyrdoms of two of the greatest saints of the early church. Yet it does not, indicating that Acts was entirely contemporary to the events and had to have been written on or around AD 62–64, within thirty years of Jesus' lifetime. And since Luke refers to his gospel as "his first book" in the very opening verses of Acts, we know that the book of Luke was written even earlier—less than thirty years after the Crucifixion. Luke wrote the book knowing it would be read by people who had been alive during Jesus' ministry, and may well have even known him.

The Gospel of Mark bears considerable similarity to Luke's and suggests one either consulted the other or both had the same source (possibly the apostle Peter), so it, too, was composed around the same time. And all four Gospels neither mention nor anticipate the Jewish Revolt and the horrifying destruction of the temple and Jerusalem in AD 70—an event no Jewish believer or Christian Gentile would possibly ignore.

So these accounts were all originally written within forty years of Jesus' earthly life. That's the equivalent of a biography of Neil Armstrong and his trip to the moon published today. Armstrong is still very much alive, as is nearly everyone who worked with him. If I were to make up stories about Neil Armstrong, you had better believe there would be an outcry of people setting the record straight and calling me a liar or a buffoon. Yet we have no such accounts from anyone regarding the content of the Gospels.

In fact, we have a contemporary account, *Jewish Antiquities*, by the Jewish historian Josephus. In it he specifically mentions Jesus, ascribes to him miraculous powers, and even goes on to mention his resurrection with a general tone of confirmation. Another account by a Jewish religious leader who opposed Christianity assigns to Jesus the ability "to perform magical acts." Julian the Apostate, a later Roman emperor who tried to take the empire back to paganism, whined that Jesus only performed his miracles in tiny villages in Judaea, and not important places like Rome.[1]

So we have not only friends of Jesus who knew him saying that he performed miracles, but also contemporary historians and even opponents who accepted these miraculous events as fact. Nobody argued the reports were lies; they just attempted to interpret the events in negative ways.

"But miracles don't happen today," you may say. Sure they do. Remember the woman I mentioned at the beginning of this book who woke up on her own after being declared clinically dead? How do we know that wasn't a miracle? We certainly can't explain it. The real complaint skeptics have is not that miracles don't happen, it's that they don't happen all the time. The skeptic thinks, *I can't do miracles. I don't know anybody who can do miracles. I've never seen a miracle happen. I can't predict a miracle. I can't explain how a miracle could work. Therefore, miracles don't happen.*

The problem with this argument is that if just anyone could perform a miracle whenever they wanted in a way that was predictable and explainable, the action wouldn't be a miracle at all. By definition, a miracle is supernatural—that is, it is something that happens *despite* the laws of nature and science as we understand them. Miracles can't be repeated or defined by science because they are outside the scope of what science can conceivably cover. They are not ordinary events or even rare events—they are extraordinary events: Healing the sick with a touch or a word. Giving sight to the blind. Opening the ears of the deaf. Restoring the leper to wholeness. Making the insane instantly sane. Feeding five thousand people with two fish sticks and five crackers. Turning water into wine. Walking on water. Silencing a raging storm. Raising the dead.

These are not the actions of science. These are not the actions of ordinary men. Just because an ordinary person like you or me can't do them or can't explain them doesn't mean they didn't happen. It just means that the person who did them is *not* an ordinary person like you or me. He is something far different. He is a person of ultimate power.

By the way, the only person in history to whom miracles are ascribed as a matter of course, acting in and of his own power, is Jesus. Everyone else derived their supposed powers from other sources. The apostles acknowledged their powers to heal came from Jesus. Moses and the prophets said their powers came from God. Jesus said he had the power because he was from God and was God.

And the founders of Buddhism, Islam, Confucianism, Hinduism, Daoism, et cetera, never demonstrated any miraculous abilities whatsoever. Not one.

So who fits the expectation of miraculous power? Jesus does. No one else.

2. Does Jesus Demonstrate Ultimate Wisdom?

Jesus' teachings were and are startlingly original. Listen to the opening lines of the Sermon on the Mount:

> And seeing the multitudes, He went up on a mountain, and when He was seated His disciples came to Him. Then He opened His mouth and taught them, saying:
>
> "Blessed are the poor in spirit,
> For theirs is the kingdom of heaven.
> Blessed are those who mourn,
> For they shall be comforted.
> Blessed are the meek,
> For they shall inherit the earth.
> Blessed are those who hunger and thirst for righteousness,
> For they shall be filled.
> Blessed are the merciful,
> For they shall obtain mercy.

> Blessed are the pure in heart,
> For they shall see God.
> Blessed are the peacemakers,
> For they shall be called sons of God.
> Blessed are those who are persecuted for righteousness' sake,
> For theirs is the kingdom of heaven." (Matt. 5:1–10 NKJV)

Those words resonate in the heart. We can't even explain all that they mean, yet somehow we *know* what they mean. We write books upon books trying to define them, and get no closer than the meaning they already achieve themselves. They are beautiful. They are profound. They are true. They are *wise.*

Jesus' wisdom confounded the wisdom of those who opposed him. The entire chapter of Matthew 22 is one long list of Jesus' replies to questions meant to trap him, with every reply instead leaving his enemies mute. His words entered into our lexicon and have become common phrases and guides for living:

> Render therefore to Caesar the things that are Caesar's, and to God the things that are God's. (Matt. 22:21 NKJV)

> But concerning the resurrection of the dead, have you not read what was spoken to you by God, saying, "I am the God of Abraham, the God of Isaac, and the God of Jacob"? God is not the God of the dead, but of the living. (Matt. 22:31–32 NKJV)

> Then one of them, a lawyer, asked Him a question, testing Him, and saying, "Teacher, which is the great commandment in the law?"
>
> Jesus said to him, " 'You shall love the Lord your God with all your heart, with all your soul, and with all your mind.' This is the first and great commandment. And the second is like it: 'You shall love your neighbor as yourself.' On these

> two commandments hang all the Law and the Prophets." (Matt. 22:35–40 NKJV)

Matthew 22 ends on this phrase: "And no one was able to answer Him a word, nor from that day on did anyone dare question Him anymore" (Matt. 22:46 NKJV).

His wisdom confounded the wisest people of his age.

Look again at the well-known instruction about loving your neighbor as yourself. In another place, Jesus phrases it as "Do to others as you would have them do to you" (Luke 6:31 NIV). You probably recognize it as the Golden Rule—in fact, I wouldn't be surprised to hear that you learned it in kindergarten, even if you never heard any other statement of Christ's in your life.

Prior to Jesus there was a phrase now known as the Silver Rule. It exists in almost all cultures, in one form or another. You've probably heard it, too: "Don't do to another what you wouldn't want done to yourself." It sounds very much like the Golden Rule, and it certainly sounds like good advice. We're not really sure who came up with it first; we might call it the world's wisdom, because it's so common. So we have the world's wisdom and Jesus' wisdom, and they both sound good. But let's put them side by side:

> Don't do to another what you wouldn't want done to yourself.
> —*The world's wisdom*

> Do to others as you would have them do to you.
> —*Jesus' wisdom*

Can you see the difference? The world's wisdom is passive. It's basically just "Leave everybody else alone." It's also negative: "Don't do this."

But Jesus' wisdom is active. It not only requires you not to harm others, but to actively help them. It's a positive, proactive call; it's the call of love.

We have to admit that if the world followed Jesus' wisdom,

the vast majority of the suffering in the world would vanish. Not only would there be no crime and no wars, there would be no crippling poverty, no starvation, no abandoned elderly, no lost children, no untreated illness, no unloved soul. Laws and politics would be unnecessary. Taxes would vanish, replaced by generosity. Government as anything other than a way to plan things together would be unneeded. We wouldn't call for tolerance because we would automatically respect the beliefs and desires of others, since we would expect that same respect ourselves. We wouldn't care about borders or race or opinions or who was at the top or who was at the bottom. We wouldn't need to, because all we would do is show love to one another.

That's Jesus' wisdom. Others have only either reproduced the Silver Rule or repeated Jesus' rule. No one has surpassed it.

3. *Is Jesus Morally Perfect?*

This is a big one. In fact, it may be the biggest one of all. Because by all indications the answer is yes. Each Gospel states that Jesus was without sin. Jesus himself left his most virulent enemies stymied by simply asking them, "Who among you can prove me guilty of any sin?" (John 8:46 NET). Nobody could even come up with one.

Can you imagine that being true of anyone else? If I said, "I dare you to mention one sin that I have done," it would be barely out of my mouth before my friends and family would clear their throats to begin the long list. How about you? Sin-free? Never lied to your boss about why you needed time off from work? Never looked at someone who wasn't your spouse and thought of something involving sex? Never picked on anyone or called them a nasty name? Never wished someone were dead? Never whacked your sister, yelled at your mother, deceptively told your father you were at the library studying when you were at a party? Never blamed God for something that was really your own fault?

I didn't think so. In fact, if I said, "Think of the worst sin you've ever committed," you'd have something in mind, even if it wasn't that big a deal. You would just know it was wrong, and that's enough. You're not morally perfect, and nobody you know is, either. Not even that handsome preacher from Connecticut.

What about all the other people in the world—even all the people in history? Can you name a sinless person? You won't find one in the big religions. Abraham tried to put one over on God by sleeping with the maid. Noah got drunk. Moses murdered an Egyptian and later disobeyed God's direct command. David cheated with Bathsheba and ordered a man murdered. Solomon worshipped idols. Mohammed broke his own marriage laws. Buddha, Confucius, and the rest never claimed moral perfection. Gandhi cheated on his wife. George Washington flogged his men. Thomas Jefferson kept slaves. It really doesn't matter whom you name in whatever position, anywhere on earth or in time, not one comes away with the sin slate completely clear.

Except Jesus.

Even his worst detractors can't point to anything he did as morally wrong. Ever. They may say they don't like what he said, but they can't call any of it sin.

And this was a man who grew up in one of the most legalistic religious cultures in the history of the world. By the time Christ was born, the Jewish culture had developed a list of rules for behavior that would make the U.S. tax code seem like a good-conduct chart for a kindergarten class. It covered things like what you could and couldn't eat or wear, how you washed your hands, whom you could talk to, what you could even see. There would be moments when just standing still with your eyes closed and your hands in your pockets would have been decried as sin according to the religious codes of the day. It was nothing short of absurd.

But Jesus stood against it. Not only did he demonstrate a sinless life amidst a culture ready to find sin in anything, he corrected that very code and pointed out how those who most pursued it were in fact guilty of sin as they did so. Can you imagine claiming a sinless life in those circumstances and having everybody actually acknowledge that you were correct in your claim?

In fact, there was only one thing Jesus' enemies could point to and call "sin"—his claim that he and God were one. But that would only be a sin if the claim were false. So far, the evidence is pointing the other way.

4. Does Jesus Exhibit Understanding and Forgiveness?

One of the most remarkable claims Jesus made during his ministry was the claim to forgive sins. Luke tells about a night Jesus was invited to dinner at the home of a wealthy and influential religious leader named Simon. All the important men in town showed up to see the latest religious sensation for themselves, to determine if he was all he was cracked up to be.

While the men were eating, a woman suddenly pushed her way past the servants and ran to Jesus. The prominent men in town were shocked; not only had a girl just barged into their private stag party, she was a well-known local prostitute! And here she was, crying at the feet of the new prophet. This party was turning out to be more interesting than they had expected.

You can imagine the mutters as the dinner guests watched this woman wet Jesus' feet with her tears and wipe them with her hair and then pour expensive perfume on him.

> Simon, the host, saw all this and harrumphed to himself, "If this man were a prophet, he would know who is touching him and what kind of woman she is—that she is a sinner."
>
> Jesus answered him, "Simon, I have something to tell you."
>
> "Tell me, teacher," he said.
>
> "Two people owed money to a certain moneylender. One owed him five hundred denarii, and the other fifty. Neither of them had the money to pay him back, so he forgave the debts of both. Now which of them will love him more?"
>
> Simon replied, "I suppose the one who had the bigger debt forgiven."
>
> "You have judged correctly," Jesus said.

> Then he turned toward the woman and said to Simon, "Do you see this woman? I came into your house. You did not give me any water for my feet, but she wet my feet with her tears and wiped them with her hair. You did not give me a kiss, but this woman, from the time I entered, has not stopped kissing my feet. You did not put oil on my head, but she has poured perfume on my feet. Therefore, I tell you, her many sins have been forgiven—as her great love has shown. But whoever has been forgiven little loves little."
>
> Then Jesus said to her, "Your sins are forgiven."
>
> The other guests began to say among themselves, "Who is this who even forgives sins?"
>
> Jesus said to the woman, "Your faith has saved you; go in peace." (Story retold from Luke 7:36–50. Quoted portion from the NIV.)

Jesus understood not only the woman and her situation, but also the thoughts and attitudes of everyone else in that room. He knew what each had done and what each needed. His host needed a rebuff for his judgmental attitude and false pretense of hospitality. The other dinner guests needed to find their alleged importance ignored. And the woman everyone else assumed was the most worthless person in the room needed to be told she was forgiven.

Jesus specialized in forgiveness. He offered it to a lonely woman at a well, to a paralytic lying on a mat, and to a woman caught red-handed in an adulterous tryst. He brought not just healing for the body, or a reprieve from earthly punishment. He brought forgiveness for the soul.

But Jesus' understanding goes far beyond just knowing what we need. Not only does he intellectually understand us, not only does he have compassion for us, but he has experienced the worst life can throw our way. He's wept at the death of a beloved friend. He's been thrown out of his hometown. He's had people hate him. He's had people try to kill him. He's been betrayed, arrested, tried, slandered, falsely convicted, beaten, scourged, spat upon, stripped naked, nailed to a cross, and mocked. What is more, he has had his own Father, the Father who loves him and whom he loves back, turn away from him to let him die.

Do you think the One who has experienced all that just might understand what you've experienced?

And remember that in the midst of all that, he looked down from the cross at the people and said, "Father, forgive them, for they do not know what they are doing."

Do we see this sort of unrestricted, unconditional forgiveness anywhere else, from anyone else? No. There's always a stopping point in other faiths. Others say, "Forgive your friends." Jesus says, "Forgive your enemies." And he did.

I'd say yes, Jesus clearly exhibits ultimate understanding and ultimate forgiveness.

5. Is Jesus Infinitely Loving?

Given what we've seen of his understanding and forgiveness, it's impossible to label Jesus as anything other than infinitely loving. When a religious leader who was curious about this new rabbi asked Jesus to explain himself, Jesus said, "For God so loved the world that He gave His only begotten Son, that whosoever believes in Him might have eternal Life" (John 3:16 NKJV). Jesus knew what he was and why he had come to earth. He was a sacrifice, offered in love, and love was why he did it.

"I have loved you with an everlasting love," God said (Jer. 31:3 NIV). And Jesus was the proof. "Greater love hath no man than this, that a man lay down his life for his friends," Jesus said (John 15:13 KJV). And then he topped it by laying down his life for those who declared themselves his enemies. Do you know what *sinner* means? It doesn't mean someone who's just been trying to have a good time and has upset the fun police. It means someone who has knowingly and willingly defied God. It means an enemy of God. It means someone who knows innately what is wrong, knows that God warned that it was wrong, and decided to do it anyway. Sound like anybody you know?

Well, then, tell me this: How would you feel if you told someone not to do something that was hurtful to you and he did it anyway? Would you feel particularly loving at that moment? I'm not asking if you'd get around to forgiving him, I'm asking right then how would you feel?

Well, how about if you pointed out his mistake, asked him again not to do it, and lo and behold, off he goes. Again. And again. And again. Getting into a less-forgiving mood now? How's that love thing working for you? With us it starts to wear a little thin, doesn't it?

But not with God. We weren't just doing it once and saying, "I'm sorry. I'll never do it again"; we were defying him over and over and over again, and never bothering to say "I'm sorry" at all. "But God demonstrates his own love for us in this: While we were still sinners, Christ died for us" (Rom. 5:8 NIV). I'd call that infinitely loving—how about you?

6. Is Jesus More Powerful Than Death?

This is the cornerstone of the Christian faith, and it's a doozy. The Resurrection of Christ. Coming back from the dead. That, my friend, is what we call a Big Deal.

There are those who try to say the Resurrection isn't important. That Christianity should just drop it, and get to the real business of sharing Christ's wisdom and leave the mystical, miraculous stuff out. Why the power of God bothers them so, I can't imagine, but if Christ's teachings were the whole point of the gospel, then I would have to say it's the bottom of the ninth with one out left and we just whiffed the second swing. Because while we have to admit that Jesus' wisdom surpasses our earthly wisdom, the truth of the matter is we can't seem to live up to it. Does this world seem like one that lives up to the Golden Rule? No, it's more like one that follows the rule of gold.

If what Jesus was about was trying to teach us to "be excellent to each other," as Bill and Ted of the excellent adventure would say, then we are in big trouble. Sure, I'll preach the Golden Rule from my pulpit and know that yes, it is a magic cure for the world's problems, but unless the people who listen to me or read this book follow it, the world is still going to be a very nasty place. We didn't need a new rule, and Jesus knew it. In fact, he said that his Golden Rule was merely the summation of the old rules that had been around since Moses. Part of it—"Love your neighbor as yourself"—is straight from Leviticus. We had that rule already. What did we need Jesus for? To remind us? Seems like a lot of trouble for what could be essentially summed up in a heavenly e-mail:

> From: God@heaven.com
> To: The_World@earth.com
> Subject: The Golden Rule
> Message: Just try it, would you?

Somehow I don't think Jesus went to all the trouble of being born of a virgin, growing up as a man, walking around Judaea doing miracles and teaching people, and then getting himself tortured and brutally executed just to say "Be nice." For that matter, even those of us who call ourselves Christians and wear WHAT WOULD JESUS DO? bracelets can't seem to pull off that advice.

So what was the real point?

The Resurrection, that's what.

To put it bluntly, if you can kill God, is he really God? On first blush, it seems like that would have to be a no. After all, God is supposed to be ultimately powerful. If I can kill God, that means I have power over God. Not only that, it also means that death has power over God, that the eternal can come to an end. If I have power over God, then he isn't God. If death has power over God, then he isn't God. If the eternal can end, then it isn't eternal.

But if you kill God and he comes back to life—whoa. Not only do I then learn I have no power over God, that even the worst I can do can't stop him, but also I learn that he is more powerful than death and that the eternal can never end.

Every gospel written puts enormous emphasis on Jesus' resurrection, and not just on the event itself, but also on Jesus repeatedly telling the disciples that it would happen. Nor was it a concept grafted on later to give Jesus some sort of "extra" authority. Remember, Mark and Luke were written within thirty years of the Resurrection. Someone would have said "Hold on" if Christians actually hadn't had it as the central component of their faith. The earliest known New Testament manuscript we have, Paul's first letter to the church in Thessalonica, repeatedly talks about Christ's resurrection as fact. Even Josephus bluntly states that Jesus rose from the dead, and mentions it as the key element of the faith: "And when Pilate, at the suggestion of the principal men amongst us, had condemned him to the cross, those that loved him at the first did not forsake him; for he appeared to them alive again the third day; as the divine prophets had foretold these and ten thousand other wonderful things concerning him. And the tribe of Christians, so named from him, are not extinct at this day."[2]

So there you have it:

Miraculous power—check
Ultimate wisdom—check
Morally perfect—check
Ultimate understanding and ultimate forgiveness—check
Infinite love—check
Power over death—check

Whether you're ready to buy into the idea that Jesus is indeed God or not, you do have to admit one thing: he certainly fits the profile.

CHAPTER 36

The God Gauntlet, Part II

WELL, DID JESUS get up from the grave? Of course, the truth is that none of us can say for sure because we weren't there. But if we examine the evidence, I believe we must conclude that he did. Four arguments have been put forth against the Resurrection of Christ, and all are based on the basic premise that people can't rise from the dead. But, again, the flaw in this thinking is revealed in the response: "You're right. Ordinary people can't rise from the dead. But Jesus wasn't ordinary." Let's take a look at the reasons people say the Resurrection didn't happen.

So Did It Happen?

1. It's All Made Up

Proponents of this theory say there was no person named Jesus.

I think we've already blown this one out of the water. It falls in the same category as moon-landing hoaxes and the Freemasons killing JFK—pure baloney. No one with any intellectual honesty seriously questions the historicity of Jesus. He lived and he died. The only point in question is whether he lived again.

2. He Didn't Really Die—He Fainted

He just fell unconscious, everybody thought he was dead, and he woke up three days later and walked home.

Frankly, the fainting argument is almost as feeble as the "no Jesus" argument. Let's look again at what happened to Jesus on Good Friday.

After his trial before Pilate, sometime before 9 A.M., Jesus was flogged with a Roman flagellum, or scourge. This was a whip with two or more leather cords in which were knotted shards of metal or bone. A particularly nasty version, called the *scorpio*, had hooks at the end designed to rip flesh off the back. It's not known which version was used on Jesus, but any version would be bad enough. The punishment was so horrible that it was illegal to use on Roman citizens. As the scourge hit Jesus, the whip tore his back to shreds within the first few blows, causing him to lose a large quantity of blood. Most victims of scourging died, even though it was supposedly not meant to be a lethal punishment.

Jesus survived the scourging, but his day didn't end there. The Roman soldiers decided to have a little fun. They shaped a crude crown out of the thorn bushes native to Palestine. These weren't rose thorns or the briars that catch you on a walk. These thorns were two-inch spikes. After dressing Jesus in this crown, probably none too gently, the soldiers mocked and repeatedly struck him on the head with a heavy staff. Have you ever heard the term "punch drunk"? That would have described the results of those head blows.

So now, in addition to massive blood loss and severe damage to his skin and back muscles, Jesus bore multiple facial contusions and was potentially suffering from a concussion with an attendant risk of permanent brain damage. At this point it was miracle enough that he was still alive.[1]

But Jesus' day was still not over. Next he was forced on a grueling march through the city, carrying a wooden beam that weighed around forty pounds. According to three of the Gospels, Jesus likely collapsed during this march, as a bystander was drafted to lug the beam to its final destination. Again, this is consistent with Jesus' weakened state due to blood loss and probable head trauma.

On reaching the hill of execution around nine in the morning, Jesus was then nailed to the cross with heavy iron spikes. These were hammered through his wrists and feet. The result would have been severe and constant pain as the spikes pressed against the central nerves running through his arms and feet. He was then left exposed for about six to nine hours, during which he had to lift his body in order to breathe. (Crucifixion suspends the body in such a way that the chest muscles prevent the lungs from working properly. Only constant effort with the legs allows the victim to exhale and inhale.) At some point Jesus ceased to lift himself, cutting off all oxygen to his body and brain. A few hours later, a soldier jammed a spear into Jesus' right side, producing a gush of blood and water, a sign that the blade had punctured Jesus' right lung and ruptured the pericardium of Jesus' heart. There was no doubt Jesus was dead.[2]

It was near sunset at this point, and Jewish law required burial before the Sabbath, which began at sundown. So Jesus was removed from the cross. His body was tightly wrapped in strips of linen, not unlike a mummy, though probably with hands and feet bound inside the wrappings and not as loose appendages. Jesus was hastily laid in an empty tomb provided by a wealthy admirer—in all probability a man-made cave in a hillside garden near the city. A massive circular stone was then rolled into a trench or track that sloped downward in front of the tomb entrance and wedged in place. The slope design allowed a few men to get the stone started so it would roll down and into place on its own, yet the immense weight of the stone prevented grave robbers from rolling it back up again. The stone itself would have completely covered the tomb entrance, leaving no handholds of any sort on the inside—just a wall of stone. According to Matthew, this stone was then sealed in place (Matt. 27:64–66). Whether that seal was physically significant we don't know, but since it was an official government seal, anyone breaking it without proper authority bore a death sentence.

With the sealing of the tomb and the placing of a Roman guard detail, Jesus' day finally came to an end.

The "he just fainted" argument assumes that despite massive blood loss, possible severe head trauma, complete oxygen deprivation for at least three hours (the length of time Jesus remained on the cross without breathing—death, of course, would have occurred in minutes), and a punctured lung and heart, Jesus simply woke up two days later without any medical attention, unwrapped himself from a first-century straitjacket, rolled a sealed stone weighing potentially a ton or more uphill (with no handholds), and chased off a squad of trained Roman soldiers. He then found a nice, clean, shiny white robe (maybe they sold them at the Jerusalem Macy's?) and tracked down his friends for a good breakfast and a laugh at the Romans. The "he just fainted" argument may deny that Christ is God, but it certainly expects him to be Superman. If you want a realistic argument, "he just fainted" is not it. Jesus didn't just take a nice, restorative nap. He died.

3. *It Was All a Hoax*

The disciples stole his body and hid it somewhere else—"Raiders of the Empty Tomb"—then told everybody that Jesus rose from the dead so they could get rich and famous.

It's actually the first argument made against the Resurrection:

> Some of the guards went into the city and reported to the chief priests everything that had happened. When the chief priests had met with the elders and devised a plan, they gave the soldiers a large sum of money, telling them, "You are to say, 'His disciples came during the night and stole him away while we were asleep.' If this report gets to the governor, we will satisfy him and keep you out of trouble." So the soldiers took the money and did as they were instructed. And this story has been widely circulated among the Jews to this very day. (Matt. 28:11–15 NIV)

One problem with this argument is that Jesus' disciples were a mishmash of workmen and scholars with no military abilities. But the guards at the tomb were Roman legionnaires, the most disciplined soldiers of the ancient world, conquerors of an empire that stretched from the shores of Britain to the sands of Arabia. The only time we read of any of the disciples fighting is when Peter takes a swipe at a Jewish servant and only manages to cut the man's ear. Basically, Peter swung at his enemy's head *and missed.* We're supposed to believe this rabble drove off Caesar's finest? That *would* be a miracle.

It would be even more of a miracle if Pilate didn't send a full cohort to track down these rebels against his authority and put them all up on their own wooden display racks. The Romans didn't mess around with people who defied their soldiers. So the "tomb raider" argument is on shaky ground already.

Others modify the "tomb raider" argument to say that the disciples didn't fight the Romans but just snuck in at night while the soldiers were sleeping. Snuck in, by the way, under total darkness and rolled that two-ton rock aside, uphill, without making any noise to wake the soldiers sleeping next to it. Jesus may not be Superman in this story, but apparently Simon Peter is.

The other problem with the "tomb raider" argument is that it assumes that the disciples could get away with the lie without facing serious consequences. But there were no First Amendment protections in the first century AD. Nobody recognized the right of free speech or religious freedom. If you said something the rulers didn't like, you could very quickly find yourself on the wrong end of a Roman sword—or as the afternoon's entertainment in the lion pit. At the very least you could be beaten, whipped, or otherwise abused until you learned to stop saying what the leaders didn't want to hear. The disciples knew this—they had just watched it happen to Jesus! He had clearly said stuff the priests didn't like, and the priests had their friend Pilate execute him. In fact, when Jesus was arrested, they all ran away and hid. Peter denied even knowing who Jesus was. Do you really think the disciples weren't aware that Jesus' fate might happen to them—in fact, very likely would?

The disciples knew what happened to people who rocked the boat. In those days, they got neither rich nor famous. They got very dead.

And that's eventually what happened to the disciples. If you look at the litany of everything that happened to them, you wouldn't bother arguing they were just "in it for themselves." They were flogged, stoned, and imprisoned. We know for certain that Peter and Paul were executed, Paul by beheading (as a Roman citizen, he could not be crucified), and Peter most likely by crucifixion. (Tradition says upside down, but no one really knows.) Other followers of Jesus died in the Roman gladiatorial games, usually being torn apart by half-starved lions. Many were crucified or set on fire. According to Acts, a prominent believer named Stephen was stoned outside the temple in full view of everyone—yet at no point did he change his story (Acts 7). Tradition has most of the twelve apostles themselves dying in various gruesome ways, though admittedly these fates are nearly impossible to prove. But given the nature of the times, these stories are possible, even likely. And the disciples certainly knew that such fates were possible from the start. They had seen floggings and stonings and crucifixions. They knew the stakes.

Yet despite these horrific dangers, not once did any disciple say, "Whoa! Put up the whips! I'm kidding. It was all just a big joke. Peter and I cooked it up to impress the chicks." The disciples *believed in* the Resurrection and stuck with that claim to the bitter end.

That seems a very odd thing to do with something you know to be a lie. Remember that Judaism was all about saying there was only one God, and the worst crime imaginable—the very one Jesus was executed for allegedly committing—was to claim that someone who wasn't God was in fact God. No Jew in his right mind would make such a claim, ever. He certainly wouldn't concoct a lie as the basis for it. Not only would he make the authorities mad at him, he would make *God* mad at him. And these guys knew what God thought of people who lied about him or said that other gods were God. The Torah and the Prophets told the fate of apostates quite clearly, and it was never good. Remember that Old Testament God who turned Sodom and Gomorrah into so much lava and set the plagues on Egypt? No Jew would dare tempt him.

4. It Was All a Psychological Hallucination

The disciples wanted to believe that Jesus rose from the dead, so they *thought* they saw him, when actually they didn't. They all suffered some sort of post-traumatic stress disorder/mass hallucination that convinced them they had seen the resurrected Christ. All 515 of them.

What? You didn't know that Christ was seen by 515 of his followers? You thought it was just his inner circle plus a few hysterical women? No, Jesus was seen by over five hundred people besides the apostles and the women in the Gospels. The apostle Paul mentions this in one of his letters, even challenging his readers to go and ask these witnesses about it, because all of them were still alive (1 Cor. 15:3–8). (That kind of kicks the "lie" argument in the gut, too. As Ben Franklin once observed, "Three can keep a secret if two of them are dead." Five hundred people aren't going to collaborate in a lie that big. Ever.)

A "mass hallucination" is a ridiculous concept. That many people simply don't imagine they see the same thing. Yes, people can misinterpret things like weather balloons and atmospheric conditions as UFOs, but that's hardly the same thing as seeing and talking to someone you know very well. The resurrected Jesus was not a mirage and he was certainly not a weather balloon.

The other flaw in the hallucination argument is that it wasn't just one appearance. All those people weren't gathered in the same place with Matthew pointing off to the distance and shouting, "Do you see him? There's Jesus! Way over there. No, by the olive tree. He's waving. Everybody wave to Jesus. Oh, he's gone. Drat. Did anybody get that on video?" Jesus wasn't the Loch Ness monster, with people all straining for one quick glimpse before he went under the waves again. According to Luke, Jesus appeared to his various disciples and followers multiple times over a period of *forty* days. He talked with them, touched them, and ate meals with them. Hallucinations don't sit down with you to share a pizza (Acts 1:3–4).

And the disciples had their own skeptic on hand to discount any "group think" case of mistaken identity. We even use his story as a synonym for skeptics today—the "doubting Thomases" of the world. When Thomas first heard his fellow disciples share the news about Jesus' resurrection, he famously said, "Unless I see the nail marks in his hand and put my finger where the nails were, and put my hand into his side, I will not believe it" (John 20:25 NIV). Thomas wasn't going to just fall in line. He wasn't going to be convinced by a fuzzy charcoal sketch or a hand waving from a passing sedan chair. He demanded the real deal.

And a week later, Jesus walked up to Thomas and said, "Put your finger here; see my hands. Reach out your hand and put it into my side. Stop doubting and believe" (John 20:27 NIV). Thomas was confronted with the physical, living, resurrected Lord, who bore proofs not only of his life but also of his death. Hallucinations don't offer to let you probe their wounds.

Jesus is not a lie. He is not a hoax or a fairy tale or a mirage. He is not a hallucination or an actor in some incredible form of first-century makeup. He is real—the resurrected Lord. The God who can defeat death. That is who Jesus is.

No other god can claim that power. All the great founders of religion are dead. You can visit Buddha's, Mohammed's, and Confucius' tombs, as well as the tombs of every other would-be prophet and god you can name. And if you pried those tombs open, inside you would find dusty bags of bones. But if you search Israel from the Golan Heights to the Sinai desert, you will not find Jesus buried there. Oh, you will find places that some call his tomb: the Church of the Holy Sepulcher (which may well be the correct site) or the Garden Tomb (which fits the description but probably isn't). It doesn't matter which, really. He's not in either one, or any other tomb you might find. He got up and left. And he's the only one to ever do so.

CHAPTER 37

Christ the Myth

SOME WOULD ARGUE that the profile of Jesus is borrowed from gods of the past—for example, the myths of Gilgamesh, Osiris, Adonis, Bacchus, or Balder. These myths, and hundreds like them, are all part of a category known as the Myth of the Dying God, which shares similarities with the myth of the Epic Hero.

The basics of the myth are simple. A god or godlike being, or a hero who is himself the son of a god and a mortal woman, sets out to bring a great power to mankind, in some cases wisdom, in others eternal life. But in the course of this quest, the god/hero learns that he must die. Sometimes it is by his own choice, sometimes he is killed by his implacable enemy. But just when the enemy thinks he has won, the god/hero rises from the dead in victory to claim his prize and save mankind from the evil fate the enemy intended.

Does that profile sound familiar to you?

There's something about this profile that continues to fascinate humankind. Maybe you recognize this story: A young boy learns he has a special heritage. He possesses powers that no one else possesses. He learns he has an enemy whom only he has the power to face. The enemy seeks to destroy the hero and the world he loves, and has the power to succeed at both. The hero selflessly faces the enemy, allowing the enemy to kill him. But just when all seems lost, the hero returns from the dead with newfound power and slays his foe, saving the world.

Harry Potter, you say? Yes. And Superman. Think Thor (if

you've seen the recent movie), Captain America, Neo of *The Matrix, Star Trek*'s Spock, Gandalf, King Arthur, and . . . Jesus.

You see, for some reason we love this story. We tell it over and over again. We'll spend hours reading books or watching movies that tell this same story. It permeates our literature, our art, and our entertainment.

"Yes, but it's all just made up!" the skeptic says. Oh, I agree. Gilgamesh et cetera, are all just made up. Fairy tales, fantasies, and myths.

But Jesus isn't.

Jesus was and is a real person. His story *isn't* made up. It actually happened. We don't just have tales and poems, we have eyewitness accounts. We have the words of people *who were actually there.* We also have the words of those who were alive at the time and heard about the events as the news of the day. These were serious, sober-minded people, telling what they saw and heard and knew so that others could know it, too. They had no concept of the Myth of the Dying God. No, they had experienced life with an extraordinary man who had done and said extraordinary things. And they had watched him die, and given up in despair—only to have him return from death to set them free.

In 1931, C. S. Lewis, who was not yet a Christian, was struggling with the made-up pagan myths and the very real fact of Jesus. Lewis wrote to a friend: "Now the story of Christ is simply a true myth: a myth working on us in the same way as the others, but with this tremendous difference that *it really happened.*"[1] It was an idea proposed to him by his close friend, J. R. R. Tolkien, a devout Catholic. Tolkien suggested that the reason Lewis so loved the stories in the ancient myths was because they were all pointing to the reality of Christ. Tolkien believed that God had planted his Son's story into the hearts of men, and men could not get away from telling it. Not long afterward Lewis concluded Tolkien was right. Christ's story was no myth. Christ's story was Truth.

Christ doesn't just fit my profile. He fits *everyone's* profile.

CHAPTER 38

Free to Choose

IF YOU CHOOSE not to put your faith in Christ, what, then, have you chosen? All the evidence that I have presented, all the profiles that Christ fits have to be cast aside. Because the other gods don't fit the profile. They aren't powerful enough, they aren't moral enough, they aren't wise enough, they aren't true enough. Pick your point, and they'll fail somewhere. And if a god fails on one point, he or she fails them all. It's 100 percent God or 0 percent God. Gods don't get graded on a curve.

The consequence is not minor. It's not about what you do on Sunday, what movies you watch, what foods you eat, or whether you pray five times a day or count worry beads. The consequence isn't whether your neighbor likes you or your favorite professor thinks you've abandoned intellectualism. The consequence isn't whether your friends decide you're no fun anymore or the girl you love says she can't marry you. The consequence isn't whether the media portrays you as a simpleton or an ogre. The consequence is eternity.

Will you be with God or won't you?

Will you be in heaven?

Or will you be in hell?

According to Jesus, it's your choice, either way.

The Choice I Make

The story of Christ has always resonated with me. When I considered other faiths, they never made sense to me. But everything I've mentioned here always has: the miracles, the moral perfection, the wisdom that is wisest of the wise, the forgiveness, the love, the Resurrection. These things have continually stirred my heart in ways I can't even express. No other god has ever even approached a close second. The scripture "He has also set eternity in the human heart" (Eccles. 3:11 NIV) describes my response perfectly. The moment I heard about Christ, I knew he was God—I knew he always had been.

As I kicked the tires of Christianity, time and again God proved himself to me. And the more I believed, the more that proof appeared. Whenever I've needed God, he has been there for me. In my struggles I've always felt his presence.

I've felt God's miraculous touch as well. A few years ago, I woke up on a Saturday morning with the overwhelming sense that I needed to pray for my son, who was then seven. I had every reason to assume he was safe. We were all at home. We lived on an access road that was really just my in-laws' driveway, so there was no traffic to worry about or strangers likely to be passing through. But I knew I had to pray for my son.

So I did. I dropped on my knees and prayed protection over my son. I had no reason to think Joey was in danger—no evidence at all—but I prayed with all my might.

As I finished my prayer—it was a quick one—I stood to go and find my son, anxious about what the danger might be. As I did, my eye caught movement through my bedroom window. I could see the end of my driveway, and I could see Joey. He was racing along in a little go-cart we had given him.

When we bought the cart, it had come with a tall orange flag attached. But that flag kept snagging on everything. I hadn't seen a point to the annoying thing; I just thought it was a nuisance, so I had ripped it off. But as I watched out my window, I learned what that flag was for—and I learned why Christ woke me up to pray.

Just as Joey darted out into the access road, my mother-in-law drove by. There was nothing I could do. She couldn't see him, he wasn't paying attention to her, and neither one could possibly hear or see me. At the very last moment, my mother-in-law slammed on the brakes—and Joey zipped past her front bumper and merrily down the road.

Why did Christ wake me to pray? Why didn't he just save Joey and let me sleep? I can't fathom God's thinking, but maybe he wanted to let me know that he does watch over me and mine. Maybe he wanted me to have an experience with him that would deepen my faith, as it certainly did. Maybe he knew that I would tell others about this experience. Maybe he knew that you would be reading this and asking your own questions. I think it's all of the above.

And yes, I said a prayer of thanks on the spot. I thanked my Christ who prompted me to pray. I thanked my Christ who listened to my prayer. And I thanked my Christ who answered that prayer. To me, that's God—the One who answers my prayer when I pray to him.

And that's Christ. My choice.

The Only Way

I know this is a hard chapter. I know it's a hard choice. It ought to be—eternity depends on it. And I know it's a hard thing to accept the notion that some ideas are wrong and some ideas are right. It's not my goal to make anyone feel bad, or to say I'm better than someone else because of what I believe.

But I'd like to share with you something that entertainer Penn Jillette shared on his video blog. Penn Jillette is an atheist and often catches flak for it from critical Christians who confuse *atheist* with *target* and *witnessing* with *open fire.* But after one show he was approached by a man who said he had a gift for him. The man complimented Jillette for his show and politely handed him a New Testament. Here's what Jillette had to say about the encounter:

> It was really wonderful. I believe he knew that I was an atheist. But he was not defensive. . . . And he was truly complimentary—it didn't seem like empty flattery. He was really kind and nice and sane, and he looked me in the eyes . . . and then gave me this Bible.
>
> And I've always said, you know, that I don't respect people who don't proselytize. . . . If you believe that there's a Heaven and Hell, and that people could be going to Hell or not getting eternal life . . . How much do you have to hate somebody to not proselytize? How much do you have to hate somebody to believe that everlasting life is possible and not tell them that? I mean, if I believed beyond a shadow of a doubt that there was a truck coming at you, and you didn't believe it, and that truck was bearing down on you, there is a certain point where I tackle you. And this is more important than that.[1]

Penn Jillette is right. There is no question more important than the question of where you will spend eternity. It's not something you get mad about because it doesn't work the way you want it to. It's not a question you put off with a vague response. What is the good of complaining about an ultimatum if the evidence says the ultimatum is simply the truth?

Put Jesus in Penn Jillette's equation. If Jesus is God and he *knows* that belief in him is the only way for us to enter heaven, doesn't love demand that he tell us that? So why be angry with him for excluding another way? He's just telling us what he knows to be the truth. If Jesus said, "Oh, it's okay to not believe this if you don't want to—you can still get to heaven," he would be lying to us. Then he would indeed be condemning us to hell while pretending to be nice. But if Jesus tells us the way to get to heaven, then he's condemning no one, any more than the mechanic who told me my brakes needed replacing was condemning me to a car crash. I'm the one who chooses whether or not to buy the brakes. I'm the one who chooses whether or not to listen to Christ. If I wind up in hell, it's not his fault. It's my choice.

CHAPTER 39

What About Those Who Have Already Died?

YOU MAY BE thinking about a loved one who has passed away. *I don't think Dad was ever a Christian. So is Frank telling me my dad is in hell?*

No, I'm not. And the reason I'm not is because *I'm not God.* Jesus is. He gets to say who's in and who's out, not me. I also don't know every moment of a person's life, and neither do you. I don't even know what Christ does between the time a person closes his eyes and opens them in eternity. If Christ wants to, he can insert himself squarely in that moment. Maybe he does. He has for some.

For example, Christ saved the thief on the cross, a story told in Luke 23. One thief mocked Christ, but the other:

> "Don't you fear God," he said, "since you are under the same sentence? We are punished justly, for we are getting what our deeds deserve. But this man has done nothing wrong."
>
> The thief then turned to Christ and said, "Jesus, remember me when you come into your kingdom."
>
> Jesus answered him, "Truly I tell you, today you will be with me in paradise." (Luke 23:40–43 NIV)

This is significant because it is a time when we are privy to the conversation between Christ and a lost soul at the very end of his life. But consider the others looking on, who can't hear Christ's words or the thief's. What would such onlookers assume about the thief's fate? Based on his life up to that point, probably that he was on an express train to hell. Even the thief admitted he deserved death. But Christ intervened, and it is only because of that one moment that we know the thief's place is in paradise.

We aren't privy to other such conversations. Maybe we think one thing about a person's final destination—and maybe Christ is doing the other. The only thing I know is that it takes Christ to offer, and us to accept, and that's between each soul and God. Neither you nor I have anything to do with it except in the choice we make in our own case.

Jesus himself warned against assuming who we would expect in heaven.

> Not everyone who says to me, "Lord, Lord," will enter the kingdom of heaven, but only the one who does the will of my Father who is in heaven. Many will say to me on that day, "Lord, Lord, did we not prophesy in your name and in your name drive out demons and in your name perform many miracles?" Then I will tell them plainly, "I never knew you. Away from me, you evildoers!" (Matt. 7:21–23 NIV)

He echoes this idea elsewhere: "But many who are first will be last, and many who are last will be first" (Matt. 19:30 NIV).

Doesn't that sound to you as if some people who have every appearance of being shoo-ins to heaven don't actually have a relationship with Jesus? And that others whose faith lives aren't showy and forceful have something stronger going on than we can see? It sounds that way to me.

We should not worry over the fates of others who have already gone. We must let the God who is in the past as well as the future concern himself with them. If we can accept that he knows best for that, then we can focus our concerns on the choices we make and the love we share with others. Love God, love people, and trust Christ. The rest will take care of itself.

The Way, the Truth, and the Life

That's how Jesus described himself: "The way, the truth, and the life" (John 14:6 NKJV).

He said he was the way to God, and the evidence supports his claim.

He said he was the truth about the universe, and his love reveals it.

He said he was the life, the key to the eternal, the doorway into heaven that anyone can enter.

"Behold, I stand at the door, and knock: if any man hear my voice, and open the door, I will come in to him, and will sup with him, and he with me" (Rev. 3:20 KJV). In the end, there is no ultimatum. There is only a promise. And the promise is true. Say yes, and enter into hope.

PART VIII

Hope

CHAPTER 40

Heavenly Oxygen

One night at the age of seventeen, I sat on my bed with my world crumbling around me. Divorce had shattered my family. My parents fought with each other, and I fought with my parents. I was filled with anger and fear. That very night I had yelled at my mother, and when my father arrived to confront me over it, the argument ended with my running to my room in tears. I sat there sobbing from the core of my soul, wondering if there was any hope at all.

And then I heard my answer. Hope spoke. A voice I had never heard before said clearly, "Don't worry, son. Everything is going to be okay."

There was no one else in the room. Just me. And God.

That night was a lesson in the two greatest truths I know: God is love, and God is hope. On that night when a teenage boy cried his heart out, God gave that boy the one thing he needed most. "Don't worry, son. Everything is going to be okay."

Hope. Second to love, it is the greatest need we have.

Worst Case or Best Case?

A book called *The Complete Worst-Case Scenario Survival Handbook* claims to be the guide for what to do in every possible extreme emergency. For example, to escape from quicksand: Carry a stout pole, and if you start to sink, lay the pole on the surface of the quicksand. Then lie on your back on the pole, and work it under your hips at a right angle to your spine. Then slowly take the shortest route to firm ground. (Note to self: Buy pole.)

To detangle a bird caught in your hair: Shield your eyes and face, grab the bird's feet from behind, pull it from your hair, and toss the bird away. Be careful not to grab the head or beak. (How to manage all this when you can't actually see the bird is not explained.)

To survive an elephant stampede: Take available cover. If there is no cover, climb a tree. If there is no tree (or you can't climb), lie down. Protect your face. (At least your friends can still identify you after you've been flattened by a herd of rampaging elephants).[1]

As fun as that book is, I'm not certain any of those things would work. But I do know that in life, to endure or escape any challenging situation—joblessness, a home foreclosure, a marriage on the rocks, addiction, the loss of a loved one—we need hope. Hope has a way of motivating us to keep pressing on no matter how hard life gets.

Eugene Lang was an East Harlem success story, a businessman and millionaire. In 1981 he accepted an invitation to speak to a class of graduating sixth-graders at the public school he had attended. But just before he spoke, the principal revealed that things had changed in East Harlem since Eugene was a student there: over 75 percent of the students he faced were unlikely to finish high school, much less attend college.

Stunned by this news, Lang made a spontaneous decision. At the end of his speech, he told the class that he would pay the college tuition of everyone there who graduated from high school. What was the result? Nearly 90 percent of the students he spoke to earned high school diplomas, and 60 percent continued on into college. With one promise, Lang more than completely reversed the principal's prediction. That's the power of hope.[2]

But hope isn't just important for educational success. Hope is fundamentally essential to life. You've probably heard the old saying "Where there's life, there's hope." Maybe so, but the greater truth is actually the opposite—where there is hope, there is life.

If you don't think so, consider this. In the 1960s, a scientist was running an experiment to see how the heart was affected by intense physical activity. He conducted the experiment by placing rats into a large tank of water from which they could not escape. Rats are extraordinary swimmers. A typical rat can swim nonstop for nearly three days, if necessary. The scientist hoped to measure the effect on their hearts of such prolonged exertion. But the researcher noticed something odd happening; many of his rats did not make the effort to swim for very long at all. Instead, the rats gave up; they literally ducked their heads under the surface and drowned themselves. He found himself dealing with a group of suicidal rats.

The researcher noticed that this event seemed to happen whenever he held a rat immobile in his hands before it was placed in the water. Yet rats that were simply dropped into the water without being held would keep swimming until they were either removed or exhausted themselves. Puzzled by this reaction, the scientist performed another experiment. This time he held the rats immobile as before and placed them in the water tank. But before the rats drowned, he rescued them. When he later returned the same rats to the water, they responded by swimming as vigorously as the rats who were never held at all.

Why was there a difference? The scientist realized that immobilizing the rats conditioned them to believe that they possessed no control over their survival—they had no hope. But the rats that had been rescued once now expected to be rescued when they entered the water, and swam in expectation of escape. They had been given back their hope. So the rats without hope drowned, while the rats with hope kept swimming. Where there was hope, there was life. Where there was no hope, life ended.[3]

This phenomenon is not restricted to rats. During the Vietnam War, the Vietcong routinely tried to entice American POWs into aiding their propaganda efforts by signing statements and participating in "reeducation" classes. The commander of one camp promised he would release any POWs who cooperated with these efforts. One young soldier at the camp agreed, doing everything his captors asked. After several months, however, the young prisoner realized the truth: the Vietcong had no intentions of letting him go, no matter what he did. When that fact hit home, the soldier gave up. He went to his cell and curled up on his cot. He wouldn't get up, he wouldn't eat, he wouldn't drink. His fellow prisoners tried to aid him, to no avail. Within a few days the boy who had been one of the healthiest prisoners in the camp was dead. Without hope, he had no life.[4]

Where there is hope, there is life. Where there is no hope, life ends.

Hope or No Hope? You Choose

When we first examined the existence of God, we encountered the arguments of atheism and addressed its weaknesses as a philosophy. But the real weakness of atheism does not arise from the conclusion it makes about God. The real flaw is in the conclusion it makes about life. You see, when you remove God from the picture, you do far more than remove the idea of a creator or a lawgiver or a righteous judge. It's easy for people to go no further than these and think, *We don't need God for that.* Those are misguided attitudes, but they overlook what atheism really rids the world of: hope.

"What do you mean, Frank? Hope doesn't need God. Hope is just a feeling." Oh, I agree that some hopes are just empty feelings. I see people pursue that sort of hope all the time. Some people put their hopes in a new job, a business, a relationship, a politician, education, money, or good looks.

But what happens to those hopes? The job stinks. The business folds. The relationship sours. The politician lies. The education doesn't impress the interviewer. The stock market collapses. The good looks turn to wrinkles, gray hair, and sagging body parts. *Poof*—hope is gone.

Under atheism, there is no point to anything. No purpose to life. No permanence to love. No value in right or wrong. No reason to do anything for others, no lasting value in doing anything for yourself. It all ends in decay and death. Here today, gone tomorrow, nobody cares. *Poof*—hope is gone.

But if hope is just a feeling, if it's only empty noise, then why is it essential to life? Why would life develop in such a way that even creatures with no more intelligence than a rat still require hope in order to live? In fact, we don't need drowning rats to tell us that hope is necessary for life. Doctors know very well that once a patient gives up hope, the odds of recovery drop dramatically. Even otherwise healthy individuals will suffer ill effects, both mentally and physically, if hope is missing from their lives. Heart disease, depression, stress, immune-system deficiencies, sleeplessness, lethargy, and even death can all result from feelings of hopelessness. Even behavioral and social problems like addiction, poverty, obesity, eating disorders, crime, and suicide can be directly linked in many cases to a lack of hope.[5]

But when hope is present, life turns around and goes the other way.

I once read a story (probably apocryphal) about a tutor who was sent to a hospital to help a young patient stay current with his schoolwork. She was not told his condition, so when she arrived at the hospital with his list of assignments, she was stunned to find her young pupil in the severe burn ward. He was wrapped from head to toe in bandages and lay listlessly on his bed. He barely acknowledged her presence.

What can I possibly do to help this boy? the tutor wondered. She couldn't do anything medically. She couldn't even tell him that everything was okay. In the end, she decided to do the only thing she could. She introduced herself, announced that they were going to study adjectives and adverbs, and began her lesson.

When her time was over, the tutor hurried home, feeling utterly useless. *What good did teaching him adjectives and adverbs do?* she wondered, fighting back tears.

The next day she got a call from the hospital. "What did you do to this boy?" the nurse demanded. Terrified that she had made his condition worse, the tutor stammered, "I just taught him about adjectives and adverbs. That's all!"

"Well, he's sitting up and asking for you," the nurse said. "Yesterday he didn't have the will to live, but today his vital signs are off the charts! You have to come back."

So the tutor did, working with the boy day after day, watching him become more and more alive with every lesson. Later she asked the boy what had happened. "Before you got here, I was sure I was dying. But when you came and started talking about adjectives and adverbs, I realized I was going to live, because the school wouldn't send you to teach adjectives and adverbs to a dying boy."[6]

Where there is hope, there is life.

What Is Hope?

Someone once said that what oxygen is to the lungs, hope is to life. But what is this essential element? We know what oxygen is: we can define it, weigh it, test it, and make it. But what is hope?

The Bible offers this stirring statement: "Now faith is the substance of things hoped for; the evidence of things not seen" (Heb. 11:1 NKJV). From this statement, the Bible goes on to list the heroes of the Jewish faith—Abel, Enoch, Noah, Abraham, Sarah, Isaac, Jacob, Joseph, Moses, Rahab—pointing out this interesting characteristic:

> All these people were still living by faith when they died. They did not receive the things promised; they only saw them and welcomed them from a distance. And they admitted that they were aliens and strangers on earth. People who say such things show that they are looking for a country of their own . . . they [are] longing for a better country—a heavenly one. (Heb. 11:13–14, 16 NIV)

A heavenly country—a promise that carried them through all of life, and a promise that was not and could not be fulfilled while they were alive.

That's a big deal. Hope is not about our past or our present, but our future. As Paul puts it: "But hope that is seen is no hope at all. Who hopes for what he already has? But if we hope for what we do not yet have, we wait for it patiently" (Rom. 8:24–25 NIV). The rats didn't keep swimming because they were already out of the water, but because they believed in the *possibility* of a way out. The burned boy didn't revive because he was already healed, or because he had been promised the best care in the hospital. He responded to the promise of a life *after* the hospital, a life in which he would need adjectives and adverbs, things he knew had no immediate medical purpose.

Hope is not a guarantee, not in the way we think of one. We try all the time to give ourselves guaranteed hope. What is a diploma, after all, except an implied guarantee: "She knows her stuff and deserves a good job." Isn't that how we think of it? How many moms and dads tell their kids to get their diplomas so they can get good jobs? Or how about marriage—don't we treat it like a guarantee? "He said 'I do,' so that means he will love me and never disappoint me and he will make certain I get flowers every day!" Right. Ever been offered a "sure thing" investment? Bernie Madoff caught a lot of supposedly smart people with that "guarantee."

The truth is that hope has no guarantees. Hope is not a present; hope is a promise. So it all comes down to whether the one making the promise can live up to his word.

So do all the people making you promises live up to their word?

How's that diploma serving you in the job market? Do you even have it on a wall somewhere so it can at least be dusted? Or is it stuck in a box in your mother's attic? Tell me, without looking, do you even know who signed it?

How about your marriage? Has Mr. Right lived up to his end of the deal, every moment, every day? Have you? I'll bet there are times when that promise has looked a little shaky on both your parts, even if things are rosy now.

How about that investment? I'll bet that's still a sore point. There's a reason three of the most despised professionals on the planet are politicians, stockbrokers, and used-car salesmen—all too often those people are about broken promises and dead hopes.

People will let you down because they're flawed and human and fallible—just like you. And if you put your hope in people, you're buying a ticket on the *Titanic*. Icebergs ahead. Better grab a life preserver.

So where can you put your hope?

Politics? Jon Stewart makes a ton of money lampooning everyone who falls for that.

Technology? Would that be jet packs, the flying car, or cold fusion?

The economy? Good luck.

Extraterrestrials? Well, if you're gonna trust in the other things I've just listed, why not go whole hog?

Yourself? I don't want to insult you, but if you're the captain of your fate, the iceberg has already hit the starboard bow. Just think of how many promises you've made to yourself and others that haven't held up. We can promise only what we can control, and there's very little in this world we can control. We have a hard enough time just controlling ourselves, much less the big questions of our future.

There's only one person, and one person ever, who consistently lives up to his promises. There is only one person who has the control to make his promises happen. There is only one source of real hope in the world. You already know his name.

Jesus.

CHAPTER 41

The Only Man of Hope

BACK WHEN BILL Clinton ran for president, his campaign put out a biographical puff film called *The Man from Hope* because the candidate happened to have been born in Hope, Arkansas. Obviously, they wanted to use this coincidence to suggest that Bill Clinton offered "hope" to the nation. But in reality that was just a slogan. There was nothing any more hopeful about Bill Clinton just because of where he was born than any other candidate. The phrase was a clever line, and that's all.

Sixteen years later, Barack Obama would pick up on the same idea and run his campaign on the slogan "Hope and Change," based on his book *The Audacity of Hope.* Like his predecessor, though, that hope was really more slogan than substance.

Notice that both candidates who ran on a platform of hope won. Why? Obviously because we all clearly desire a future filled with hope—a message of hope resonates with all of us. But the truth is, no matter what you think of their politics, neither man actually possessed the ability to offer real, lasting hope. Policies and political promises, yes. But real hope? No.

There is only one Man of hope, and his hope lasts through far more than an election campaign. His hope doesn't just change government policies—it changes lives.

Here's how he changed the life of one woman. After a visit to Jerusalem, Jesus decided to return to Galilee, which lay to the north past a region known as Samaria. Samaria was populated by the descendants of Israelites who had intermarried with Assyrian conquerors eight hundred years before Christ. The Jews of Galilee and Judaea considered the Samaritans to be traitors and half-breeds. The two ethnic groups also disagreed on religious grounds, with the Jews claiming the only holy temple was in Jerusalem, while the Samaritans said that the only true temple was on Mount Gerizim, in the middle of Samaria. The dislike between them was about at the level of that between Palestinians and Israelis today.

There were four established routes between Galilee and Jerusalem, and only two went through Samaria. Jews would usually take a route that crossed the Jordan River so as to avoid Samaria. These routes were well-known and reasonably safe, so there was no real reason for Jesus to choose the route that went through the heart of Samaria. But Jesus had an appointment that was more important than political squabbles or doctrinal differences. He had an appointment to offer hope.

The Bible tells how he stopped to rest at a well outside of a Samaritan town and sent his disciples to buy food. As he rested, a woman approached the well to draw water. The passage makes a point that she came at noon, during the high heat of the day. In those days it was odd to draw water at noon, because women typically went to the well early in the morning, before the sun was fully up. They drew all their water for the day so they did not have to return when it was hot. But this woman came not when the other women were there, but at noon, when everyone else in the village would be in the cool of their homes.

As the story continues, we learn that Jesus knew why the woman avoided the others. "You have had five husbands, and the man you are with now is not your husband," he said to her. It's not hard to guess that her desire to be alone at the well was because everyone in the village knew her life story. You can imagine the whispers about her: the scowls of the women, the frowns of the men (with probably a few leers mixed in). Whether she felt shame or was just sick of the ill-treatment, the Bible doesn't say, but she certainly didn't want to be around anyone. So imagine her surprise and wariness when she saw a stranger sitting at the well at high noon.

We can picture her, trudging down the road from the village, carrying her big earthen jar, staring down at the dirt track to keep her eyes out of the glare of the sun. She knows the way; she has no need to look ahead, no desire to look behind. She knows what awaits at both places: a well of slightly brackish water and a long trudge back to the home of a man who treats her like a piece of property. If she is lucky, she will see no one who will spit at her. She is the rat swimming in the pool with no way out, waiting for the day she drowns.

As she reaches the well, she feels something is different. For the first time she looks up. She is not alone! A man is watching her: a Jew, no less, to whom she is an unclean half-breed. His clothes are finer than any she has ever worn, and he bears the tassels of a rabbi, a teacher of the law that condemns her. *What is he doing here?* she wonders. She's sure he will show her far worse hate than any she has seen in town. In a moment, she knows, his face will grimace in disgust. He will rise and walk away, or worse, he may throw stones at her. But it is too late now. She has walked a long way. She cannot turn back without her water—she needs it to prepare the evening meal, for her man will berate and beat her if it is not ready. Maybe this rabbi will be one of the kinder sorts and just ignore her as if she were a passing dog. She moves up to collect her water.

And then the strange man speaks to her, and in a few moments of conversation everything changes. Her entire world spins upside down and inside out. She runs back to town, not caring about the heat or the dust of the road or the light of the sun as it falls on her exposed arms and legs. She leaves behind the water jug, unafraid of her man and his displeasure about his dinner. She shouts to the village, to the very people who despise her, whom she has avoided at all costs until now. She can't wait to share what has happened. She doesn't care what they think of her. She doesn't care if they're inside, resting and eating out of the sun.

She has to tell them—and she asks them all to come back to the well with her, to meet this amazing stranger with his bold and powerful words.

And they do—all of them! The entire village, from the elders to the women to the man who keeps her as his mistress, they all rush to see the One she has met, so startling and compelling is the change in her.

What is that change?

It's hope.

Who gave it to her?

Jesus.

If you read the story from John 4, the things Jesus said to the woman had nothing at all to do with her current life except when he revealed his miraculous knowledge of her personal story. He didn't promise to relieve her current troubles at all. He didn't promise to turn her lover into the perfect husband, or make the townswomen respect her, or for that matter give her an education, a good job, or financial security. In fact, he spoke as if none of that was important at all. The only thing he offered her was this: "Everyone who drinks this water [from the well] will be thirsty again, but whoever drinks the water I give him will never thirst. Indeed, the water I give him will become in him a spring of water welling up to eternal life" (John 4:13–14 NIV). That's the hope of eternal life, a life worshipping the Father "in spirit and in truth" (John 4:24 NIV).

As far as Jesus was concerned, it was the only hope that mattered. It trumped all the others. And for the woman, that's exactly what it did. It was the hope that her life, that her past, was not a barrier between her and God. That God knew her fully and offered himself to her anyway. That's what changed her attitude. No other promises were offered because no other promises were needed. She saw that the life she was drowning in had a way out—and suddenly she could swim again. Suddenly, she could live. That is the result of the hope Jesus offered.

Everywhere Jesus went, he offered that hope. To the paralytic he said, "Your sins are forgiven." To the woman who washed his feet with her tears, he said, "Your sins are forgiven." To the thief next to him on the cross, he offered paradise. Even to those who crucified and mocked him, he offered the same forgiveness, the same hope. When John saw the empty tomb, he found hope. When Thomas saw the risen Lord, he found hope. When Peter cried before his Lord on the rocky beach in Galilee, Jesus erased the disciple's words of failure and denial and gave him hope.

He gave hope to Stephen, and the dying Stephen looked up to see his hope fulfilled.

He gave hope to Paul on the road to Damascus, and Paul clung to it through beatings, storms, prison, and death.

But he didn't stop. Jesus has given hope to people every day since. He never stops giving it.

Not long ago I had the opportunity to tour Lakewood Church in Houston, Texas, home of my fellow pastor Joel Osteen. The tour was led by the children's pastor, Craig Johnson. At one point in the tour we came to an area called the Champions Club, which is specifically designed to minister to special-needs kids. These rooms housed specialized sensory equipment and physical-fitness equipment for these children, who may have physical or developmental challenges such as cerebral palsy or autism. As we toured this area, I noticed an unusual passion in Craig's voice. It seemed to be more than just a natural compassion for the children, and I wondered at its source. Just before the tour ended, I found out why.

Craig has a son named Connor, who at five years old was diagnosed with autism. The diagnosis came after Craig and his wife, Samantha, began to notice that their son had never spoken a full paragraph and didn't speak in complete sentences. He would speak a phrase here or there, but Connor had never put a complete thought together.

Craig and Samantha refused to let Connor's struggles diminish their faith in God or their little boy. Every day they would speak that faith into little Connor, telling him that he was more than a conqueror, that he could do all things through Christ. At bedtime every night, they would read to him and pray with him.

At first, Craig shared all this in a matter-of-fact tone. But then his voice started to crack. As his eyes filled with tears he said, "One night, when my wife was about to turn off the lights in Connor's room, she heard him start speaking. He went on and on, speaking clearly and fluently. She ran to get the video camera to record the first sentences Connor had ever spoken in his life." By this time, tears were rolling down Craig's cheeks.

And then Craig told me, verbatim, the first paragraph little Connor ever said: "This is my Bible. I am what it says I am. I have what it says I have. I can do what it says I can do. Today I will be taught the Word of God. I boldly confess my mind is alert, my heart is receptive; I will never be the same. I am about to receive the incorruptible, indestructible, ever-living seed of the Word of God. I will never be the same, never, never, never. I'll never be the same, in Jesus' name."

Craig went on to explain that Connor will watch cartoons only for three minutes at a time without fussing. But he will sit down and watch Joel Osteen's videotaped messages without making a sound for half an hour at a time.

As I looked in Craig's eyes as he told this story, I saw Jesus' brand of hope in action. I saw hope that was an anchor to Craig's soul. I saw one of the greatest gifts that God has offered humankind. I saw the gift of hope, given by God to Craig and Samantha Johnson—a gift expressed in the words of five-year-old Connor.

It's not the gift of a cure. Connor still has autism. It's not the gift of understanding. Connor still faces all the struggles to communicate that are common to children with his condition. No, what I saw in Craig's eyes was something far greater and more lasting. I saw a hope that wasn't just for this life, but for something far more precious—a hope that Connor would know his God, not just now, but forever.

CHAPTER 42

The Greatest Hope of All

AND NOW WE'VE come to the whole point.

You know it. You've been reading about it all along—the greatest hope of all.

The hope that life is indeed more than just random interactions of purposeless particles.

The hope that you are more than just a souped-up monkey.

The hope that the universe has a reason for being, and that you yourself have a reason for being within it.

The hope that your purpose, your existence, your reason to be lasts beyond just the here and now, the gritty, lousy, harsh, hard, clumsy realities of this broken world.

It is the hope that God loves you. The hope that he has planned a future for you, in eternity, with him. The hope that you will live forever in love, being loved and giving love in return. The hope that this life is not all there is, that everything does not end in death and decay and pointlessness.

One of Jesus' greatest miracles occurred just before his own death. Short of his own resurrection, it may be the single greatest miracle he performed. Jesus was in Galilee when word came to him that a very dear friend, Lazarus, was fatally ill. Lazarus had two sisters, Mary and Martha, who were also friends and followers of Jesus. It's clear from the story that Mary and Martha were the source of the message, and that they wanted Jesus to come heal their brother.

But for reasons that are never explained, Jesus delayed his

trip. Keep in mind that it would take several days to walk from Galilee to Bethany, just outside Jerusalem, where Lazarus, Mary, and Martha lived. So Jesus' delay was surprising to everyone: Did he not know that time was of the essence? Finally, Jesus chose to set out and told his disciples that Lazarus was sleeping. *Aha!* they thought. *See, Jesus knew the disease wasn't fatal.* One of them even praised the news, saying, "Well, if he's sleeping, that means he can rest and will get better." Jesus just shook his head. "I mean he's dead, guys." I'll bet that put a damper on the conversation for the trip.

When Jesus arrived in Bethany, Martha came up the road to meet him. Like the others, she didn't understand the delay. She even chastised Jesus, at least obliquely: "Lord, if you had only been here, Lazarus would not have died." Jesus replied, "Your brother will rise again." Martha treated this pretty much as you or I would have—as a statement about heaven: "I know he will rise again in the resurrection at the last day." And then Jesus said something to her that was striking, and not at all what she or anyone else was expecting: "I am the resurrection and the life. He who believes in me will live, even though he dies; and whoever lives and believes in me will never die. Do you believe this?" (John 11:25–26 NIV).

It is the ultimate statement of hope and the ultimate claim—that death is not the end, because Jesus has power over death. And Jesus then proved it by raising Lazarus from the dead.

Jesus had raised people before, but those had all been deathbed resurrections, the sort of miracles that anyone might point at and say, "Oh, they weren't really dead. They were just unconscious, and Jesus did a little first-century CPR." But Lazarus was different. Lazarus had been dead for at least four days: he'd been wrapped, buried, and sealed in a tomb. The Bible indicates that his body had started to decay; Martha even warned Jesus about the stench from Lazarus' grave. And yet when Jesus commanded Lazarus to come out, the dead man walked out. The power of Jesus was shown to extend beyond illness, beyond death, beyond decay. They are not the end at all. With Jesus, there is no end.

And that is the greatest hope of all.

Personal Lessons in Hope

Three people showed me what that hope truly means. Their names are John Nuzzi, John Gilbert, and Jodi Lynn.

John Nuzzi taught me that hope through a testimony he sent our church after his father's death. That letter read:

> I love telling the story about the end of the movie *It's a Wonderful Life.* All of Jimmy Stewart's friends come over to his home on Christmas Eve to pitch in funds to make up for the devastating loss of a missing deposit from the community bank he runs. . . .
>
> Clarence the angel is looking down on the scene of the Jimmy Stewart character surrounded by scores of loving friends coming to his rescue and says the final line of the movie: "No man is a failure who has friends." I can't help but think of my dad. To judge him by that standard, he was the most successful man I ever knew!
>
> I owe a debt of gratitude to Pastor Frank and Faith Church for leading my father to welcome Jesus into his heart, and accept him as his Lord and Savior to become born again. I rest assured I will see him again.
>
> Your brother in Christ,
> John N. Nuzzi

John Gilbert and his wife, Sherrill, were longtime members of our church. She was always more extroverted while he was quiet. Cheryl worked in our elder care and women's ministries, and John served as an usher. He was a man of very few words, but the last years of his life spoke to me in volumes. After several years of serving in our church, John came down with Alzheimer's disease. Slowly but surely, he started to lose his memory. But in all that time, he kept coming to church, and he always remembered who I was. He would give me a big hug, shake my hand, and tell me it was good to see me. And I knew that he meant it. And he always said, even to the very end, "Jesus is my Lord." Even though he and Sherrill knew that John was going to die, they had this remarkable peace about them, a confidence and courage wrapped up in John's remembered phrase, "Jesus is my Lord."

Jodi Lynn was born with spina bifida, a birth defect of the spinal cord. Because of complications of her condition, both of her legs had been amputated. I knew her as a young woman in her twenties, a faithful and joyful member of our church. Though she loved the Lord, she always had questions for me about why her life had turned out the way it had. Answering such things is not a task for fainthearted pastors! But even with the difficulties she faced, she was one of the brightest and happiest young women you would ever meet. Her favorite role in life was being an aunt to her sister's daughters.

Unfortunately, as a result of her spina bifida, which left her susceptible to illness, Jodi Lynn became gravely ill. The illness had her in and out of the hospital, and we all feared that her body would not be able to fight off the latest attack. But in the midst of this she came to me at church and said, "Pastor Frank, I don't know if I'm going to make it. But I know one thing—I'm going to be with Christ forever and ever." She said it with no fear or sadness. She wasn't choked up. There was no trembling and no regret.

It was the most positive statement I had ever heard—without any fear whatsoever. She just *knew* that she didn't have to face death alone. She understood that Christ was her Savior, and it gave her an overwhelming peace to face death courageously.

Look back at their words:

"I rest assured I will see him again."
"Jesus is my Lord."
"I'm going to be with Christ forever and ever."

John Nuzzi, John Gilbert, and Jodi Lynn had heard the promise of Christ. They heard it and believed it. And death lost all its power for them. Amidst grief, John Nuzzi found a promise of reunion. Amidst the fading of his mind, John Gilbert found a promise of renewal. Amidst weakness and death, Jodi Lynn found the promise of new strength in a new life.

Now Jesus is repeating that promise to you. The promise he made to the woman at the well. The promise he made to Peter and Paul and John and Thomas and Matthew and Mark and James, and all the others who gathered around him so long ago. The promise he made to Martha and Mary. The promise he called out to Lazarus while he was in the grave. The promise he made to me. The promise he offers you: "I am the resurrection and the life. He who believes in me will live, even though he dies; and whoever lives and believes in me will never die. Do you believe this?"

Do you?

In the end, it's the only question that matters, and the answer is entirely up to you.

Death or Life.

God doesn't make the choice—you do.

The Choice You Can Make

It really is as simple as that. There's no magic formula, no hoop to jump through, no laborious effort or excruciating sacrifice. That's all been done. Your choice to accept the gift Christ offers is nothing more or less than a choice to acknowledge that you need him, that he is who he says he is, that he did what he says he did, and that he did it for you. There are many ways to accept this gift. In my church, we suggest a prayer something like this:

Heavenly Father, today I give my heart completely and wholly to you. I recognize that I'm flawed and broken by my own choices, my own actions, my own pride. I cannot fix these flaws myself; I need a Savior. Therefore I invite Jesus Christ to be the Lord of my life. I accept and put my faith in the work he finished on the cross, recognizing that he died in my place, and rose again to offer me life now and forever.

Thank you, Jesus, for the price you paid on the cross and the victory you won in your resurrection from the dead. And thank you, Father, for receiving me as your child. From this day forward I vow to glorify you with my life as you reveal my purpose for living to me.

In Jesus' name I pray. Amen!

The exact words really don't matter. It is important only that the prayer comes from your heart. As Paul said, "If you declare with your mouth, 'Jesus is Lord,' and believe in your heart that God raised him from the dead, you will be saved. For it is with your heart that you believe and are justified, and it is with your mouth that you profess your faith and are saved" (Rom. 8:9–10). There is nothing in life more simple, nothing in life more important, and nothing in life more profound. Open your heart, speak with your mouth, and live.

Acknowledgments

Lisa, my wife, for your love and unending support—I love you.

Nicole and Joseph, my kids; on the book you weren't much help, but in life you guys make it all worth it.

Mom and Dad, other than God, I owe much of what I am to you.

Howard, you are the man!

Holly, thanks for the edits.

Faithafarians, aka my amazing congregation, you inspire me.

Dana, my assistant, you make life easy for me.

My staff—like Moses and his staff, together we can part the Red Sea.

Notes

Chapter 3: Religion, Politics, and Death

1. Testimony of Harold S. Bride, British Wreck Inquiry Commission, day 14. The relevant section begins at 16663. Available at www.titanicinquiry.org/BOTInq/BOTInq14Bride04.php.
2. Testimony of Edward Wilding, British Wreck Inquiry Commission, day 19. The relevant section begins at 20266. Available at www.titanicinquiry.org/BOTInq/BOTInq19Wilding02.php.
3. Ibid.

Chapter 4: Grandma Wasn't There

1. "Husband Celebrates Miracle as 'Brain Dead' Wife Wakes Up in Hospital," May 11, 2011, Fox News, www.foxnews.com/health/2011/05/11/husband-celebrates-miracle-brain-dead-wife-wakes-hospital/.

Chapter 5: Outside Evidence

1. For a layman-friendly discussion of M-theory, read Carlos Herdeiro, "M-theory, the theory formerly known as Strings" from the Cambridge Relativity Web site, University of Cambridge, copyright 1996, www.damtp.cam.ac.uk/research/gr/public/qg_ss.html#mtheory.

   Please note that M-theory and its parent theory, string theory, are highly speculative and technical in nature, have not been confirmed by experimentation (which may not even be possible), and should not be taken as scientific fact.
2. P. M. H. Atwater, "17 Near-Death Experience Accounts from 'Beyond the Light'" (New York: Birch Lane Press, 1994, paperback reprint by Avon Books, New York City, 1995), as quoted on the International Association for Near Death Studies Web site, iands.org/nde-stories/17-nde-accounts-from-beyond-the-light.html.

   Hemingway's story is number 6 on this list.
3. From www.near-death.com/famous.html, account excerpted from Jean Ritchie, *Death's Door: True Stories of Near-Death Experiences* (New York: Dell, 1996).
4. Sam Parnia, MD, PhD, *What Happens When We Die: A Groundbreaking Study with the Nature of Life and Death* (Carlsbad, CA: Hay House, 2006), 73.

5. Ibid., 52–53.
6. Jeffrey Long, MD, with Paul Perry, *Evidence of the Afterlife: The Science of Near-Death Experience* (New York: HarperCollins, 2010), 5–7.
7. Sam Parnia, *What Happens,* 11.
8. Jeffrey Long, *Evidence,* 149–71.
9. Sam Parnia, *What Happens,* 9–10.
10. Ibid., 21–28, 84–97.
11. Ibid., 22.
12. Ibid., 121, 152–59.

Chapter 6: Inside Evidence

1. Kenneth E. Hagin, *Man on Three Dimensions* (Tulsa, OK: Kenneth Hagin Ministries/RHEMA Bible Church, 1973, 15th printing, 1991), 8.

Chapter 7: Hey, That Looks a Lot Like Me

1. Parnia, *What Happens,* 75.

Chapter 8: God or No God?

1. Christopher Hitchens, *God Is Not Great: How Religion Poisons Everything* (New York: Twelve/Hachette Book Group, 2007). Chapter titles are taken from table of contents.
2. "Dawkins Says Religion Is 'Like Sucking a Dummy,'" by the Times Online (London), reposted by Richard Dawkins Foundation for Reason and Science Web site, March 28, 2007, richarddawkins.net/articles/810-dawkins-says-religion-is-39-like-sucking-a-dummy-39.

Chapter 9: Big Bang or Intelligent Designer?

1. Paul Davies, *The Mind of God: The Scientific Basis for a Rational World* (New York: Simon & Schuster, 1992), 16.
2. Sir Fred Hoyle, "The Universe: Past and Present Reflections," *Engineering & Science,* November 1981, 8–12. The article in which he made this conclusion can be found at calteches.library.caltech.edu/3312/1/Hoyle.pdf.

Chapter 10: Who Made God?

1. George F. R. Ellis, "Does the Multiverse Really Exist?" *Scientific American* 305, no. 2 (August 2011).

Chapter 11: My Right, Your Wrong

1. Lt. Col. Don Grossman,"Hope on the Battlefield," summer 2007, greatergood.berkeley.edu/article/item/hope_on_the_battlefield/.
2. The concept of the Innate Moral Law is derived from the thinking of C. S. Lewis, expressed in his classic work *Mere Christianity.* He delves even deeper into the concept there, and I highly recommend it for further reading.

Chapter 12: Could So Many People Be Lying?

1. John W. Loftus, ed., *The Christian Delusion: Why Faith Fails* (Amherst, NY: Prometheus Books, 2010).

Chapter 13" What We Can't See Is Real

1. "Americans Describe Their Views About Life After Death," The Barna Group, October 21, 2003, www.barna.org/barna-update/article/5-barna-update/128-americans-describe-their-views-about-life-after-death.
2. Ibid.

Chapter 14: Visions of Hell

1. Maurice Rawlings, MD, *Beyond Death's Door* (New York: Bantam, 1981), 1–6.
2. Josephine Vivaldo, "Former Non-Christian: My Time in Hell," *The Christian Post*, May 3, 2011, www.christianpost.com/news/former-atheist-my-time-in-hell-50071/.

Chapter 15: So Why Is Hell So Hard to Believe?

1. Leonard Ravenhill, *Why Revival Tarries* (Minneapolis, MN: Bethany Fellowship, 1960), 19.
2. Lee Strobel, *The Case for Faith: A Journalist Investigates the Toughest Objections to Christianity* (Grand Rapids, MI: Zondervan, 2000), 172.

Chapter 16: Why Hell?

1. Thomas Jefferson, *Notes on the State of Virginia, Query XVIII*, 1781, 272. Available at www.pbs.org/jefferson/archives/documents/frame_ih198149.htm.

Chapter 17: Three Bad Words

1. Lee Strobel, *The Case for Faith*, 185, quoting from John Stott and David L. Edwards with response from John Stott, *Essentials: A Liberal-Evangelical Dialogue* (London: InterVarsity, 1989), 316.

Chapter 19: The Choice

1. C. S. Lewis, *The Problem of Pain* (New York: Touchstone, 1996), 114.
2. ———, *The Great Divorce* (New York: HarperOne, 2001), 75.

Chapter 20: The Scientist and the Little Boy

1. Ian Sample, "Stephen Hawking: 'There Is No Heaven; It's a Fairy Story,'" *The Guardian*, May 15, 2011, www.guardian.co.uk/science/2011/may/15/stephen-hawking-interview-there-is-no-heaven.
2. Todd Burpo with Lynn Vincent, *Heaven Is for Real: A Little Boy's Astounding Story of His Trip to Heaven and Back* (Nashville, TN: Thomas Nelson, 2010), 154.
3. Ibid., xvii–xxi.
4. Ibid., 65, 67, 72, 86–87, 94–97, 100–3, 120–21.

Chapter 23: Our Here Affects Our There

1. Todd Burpo, *Heaven,* 72.

Chapter 28: Live Now

1. John Maxwell, *Today Matters* (Nashville, TN: Warner Faith, 2004), 13–14, cited as an e-mail from Dale Witherington, April 24, 2003.

Chapter 30: Live People

1. Erin O'Donnell, "How to Forgive Your Enemies (Your Hate Is Only Hurting You)": *Natural Health* 32, no. 9 (December 2002), 52 (4). "Long-standing disputes can stress you out, increase your risk of heart disease, and even trigger headaches and back pain. Free yourself and feel better."
2. TerriLynn McDonough, video testimony, available from Kerry and Chris Shook at the One Month to Live: 30 Day Challenge Web site: www.onemonthtolive.com/includes/videos/stories_terrilynn.html.
3. Ibid.

Chapter 31: Live Loved

1. Richard Hack, *Hughes: The Private Diaries, Memos and Letters* (Beverly Hills, CA: New Millennium Entertainment, 2001), 1–19 (condition at death, causes), 302 (wealth).

Chapter 35: The God Gauntlet, Part I

1. Flavius Josephus (AD 37?–101?), *Jewish Antiquities,* book 18, chapter 3, paragraph 3.

> Now there was about this time Jesus, a wise man, if it be lawful to call him a man; for he was a doer of wonderful works, a teacher of such men as receive the truth with pleasure. He drew over to him both many of the Jews and many of the Gentiles. He was [the] Christ. And when Pilate, at the suggestion of the principal men amongst us, had condemned him to the cross, (9) those that loved him at the first did not forsake him; for he appeared to them alive again the third day; (10) as the divine prophets had foretold these and ten thousand other wonderful things concerning him. And the tribe of Christians, so named from him, are not extinct at this day.

From Christian Apologetics & Research Ministry, "Non-biblical accounts of New Testament events and/or people," carm.org/non-biblical-accounts-new-testament-events-andor-people.

The Talmud

> On the eve of the Passover Yeshu [Jesus] was hanged [a euphemism for crucifixion]. For forty days before the execution took

> place, a herald went forth and cried, "He is going forth to be stoned because he has practiced sorcery and enticed Israel to apostasy. Any one who can say anything in his favour, let him come forward and plead on his behalf." But since nothing was brought forward in his favour he was hanged on the eve of the Passover!

This quotation was taken from the reading in *The Babylonian Talmud,* translated by Isidore Epstein (London: Soncino, 1935), volume III, Sanhedrin 43a, 281, as cited in Gary R. Habermas, *The Historical Jesus: Ancient Evidence for the Life of Christ* (Joplin, MO: College Press, 1996). The relevant chapter can be found online at the author's Web site: www.garyhabermas.com/books/historicaljesus/historicaljesus.htm#ch9.

Julian the Apostate,* Against the Galileans, *Book I

> Yet Jesus, who won over the least worthy of you, has been known by name for but little more than three hundred years: and during his lifetime he accomplished nothing worth hearing of, unless anyone thinks that to heal crooked and blind men and to exorcise those who were possessed by evil demons in the villages of Bethsaida and Bethany can be classed as a mighty achievement.

From Julian the Apostate, *Against the Galileans:* remains of the three books, excerpted from Cyril of Alexandria, *Contra Julianum* (1923), 319–43, translated by Wilmer Cave Wright, PhD. Available at www.tertullian.org/fathers/julian_apostate_galileans_1_text.htm.

2. Flavius Josephus, *Antiquities.*

Chapter 36: The God Gauntlet, Part II

1. The various beatings received by Jesus are detailed in the Gospels:

Struck in the face with fists and slaps during trial: Matthew 26:67–68, Mark 14:65, Luke 22: 63–65 (John does not mention this incident).

Scourged, crowned in thorns, beaten in the head and/or face: Matthew 27:26–31, Mark 15:15–20, John 19:1–3 (Luke does not mention these events).

That the result of the head blows would have been severe bruising at the least and a concussion or even internal, permanent brain trauma is consistent with the typical effects of repeated head blows as listed by the National Institutes of Health on their Web site: www.nlm.nih.gov/medlineplus/ency/article/000028.htm.

Tradition suggests the crown of thorns was made from the "Christ's Thorn" jujube plant, native to Palestine and mentioned in the Old Testament as well (Judges 9:7–15, with some irony), although there are other native thorn plants that might have been used.

The effects of scourging, particularly severe blood loss, can be found in:

William D. Edwards, MD; Wesley J. Gabel, MDiv; Floyd E. Hosmer, MS, AMI, "On the Physical Death of Jesus Christ," *Journal of the American Medical Association* 255, no. 11 (March 21, 1986), 1455–63. This article includes medical illustrations of the wounds Jesus would have received from the scourging, crucifixion, and spear thrust, and is quite graphic in nature.

2. William D. Edwards, Wesley J. Gabel, and Floyd E. Hosmer, "On the Physical Death."

Chapter 37: Christ the Myth

1. C. S. Lewis, letter to Arthur Greeves, 1931, quoted in Alan Jacobs, *The Narnian: The Life and Imagination of C. S. Lewis* (New York: HarperCollins, 2005), 148–49.

Chapter 38: Free to Choose

1. Penn Jillette, "Encounter with a Christian fan." This video clip is available online from many sources. Among the most reliable to retain it in archives is Breitbart TV: tv.breitbart.com/atheistmagician-penn-jillette-describes-remarkable-encounter-with-christian-fan/.

Chapter 40: Heavenly Oxygen

1. Joshua Piven and David Borgenicht, *The Complete Worse-Case Scenario Survival Handbook* (San Francisco: Quirk Productions/Chronicle Books, 2007), 197–98 (quicksand), 38 (bird), 48–50 (elephants).
2. History of the "I Have a Dream" Foundation, http://www.ihaveadreamfoundation.org/html/history.htm.
3. Martin Seligman, "Submissive Death: Giving Up on Life," *Psychology Today*, May 1973, 80–85.
4. Ibid.
5. Sources for the health and societal effects of hopelessness are numerous, and include the following studies:

   Mary O. Whipple, BA; Tené T. Lewis, PhD; Kim Sutton-Tyrrell, DrPH; Karen A. Matthews, PhD; Emma Barinas-Mitchell, PhD; Lynda H. Powell, PhD; Susan A. Everson-Rose, PhD, MPH, "Hopelessness, Depressive Symptoms, and Carotid Atherosclerosis in Women: The Study of Women's Health Across the Nation (SWAN) Heart Study," stroke.ahajournals.org/content/40/10/3166.full.pdftthml.

   "Unnatural Causes," PBS, interview with David R. Williams, Norman professor of public health, professor of African and African American studies and sociology at Harvard University, executive director of the Robert Wood Johnson Foundation Commission to Build a Healthier America. While this interview deals primarily with racial disparities in health between whites and blacks in America, one cause cited is a disparity of hope between the two groups. www.unnaturalcauses.org/assets/uploads/file/davidwilliams.pdf.

Martin E. P. Seligman, "Positive Health," *Applied Psychology: An International Review,* 2008, 57, 3–18, http://www.ppc.sas.upenn.edu/positivehealth2008article.pdf.

"Positive Health: An Overview," Authentic Happiness Web site, Positive Psychology Center, University of Pennsylvania, Martin Seligman, director: www.authentichappiness.sas.upenn.edu/newsletter.aspx?id=1559.

Other abstracts regarding the effects of hopelessness (or "learned helplessness" as defined in current psychological theory) can also be found at the Positive Psychology Center: www.ppc.sas.upenn.edu/cvabs.htm.

6. There are several versions of this story on the Internet, which is where we found it. One version is here: www.fjm.org/news_events/media_center/take_2/20110816.

After You Die:

Unveiling the Mysteries of Heaven

FRANK SANTORA

Reading Group Guide

No one likes to talk or think about death. It's the ultimate reality of life; however, it is a topic often ignored or pushed aside. In *After You Die: Unveiling the Mysteries of Heaven,* Pastor Frank Santora tackles head-on the issue of death, offering cultural, scientific, philosophical, and biblical evidence to unveil both the truth about the afterlife and the key to living a life with greater purpose.

For Discussion

1. What's your immediate response when the topic of death comes up? How would you describe our culture's attitude toward death?

2. Before reading *After You Die,* what were some of your default assumptions about what happens after you die? Were any of those assumptions challenged or changed as a result of reading this book? If so, which ones?

3. Have you experienced the death of someone close to you? How did the reality of death impact you? Did it raise any questions that you hadn't considered before? If so, what were they? How did you address or respond to those questions?

4. In chapter 6, Santora describes the difference between our body, soul, and spirit. How would you describe a "soul"? How is it different from your physical body? What about your "spirit"?

5. Santora quotes Genesis 2:7 where God breathes life into Adam: "And then [he] breathed into his nostrils the breath

of life; and man became a living being." Read this verse out loud. What does this say about life and death? Who is giving life? Who is receiving life? What questions or struggles does this verse raise for you, if any?

6. In your opinion, what is the difference between evidence and proof of God's existence? What pieces of evidence does Santora provide for God's existence?

7. Have you ever known anyone who reported being dead for a brief period and then came back to life? What was your response to the claims of near death experiences (NDEs) described in *After You Die*? Santora quotes findings from a 1982 survey that over eight million people in the United States reported near death experiences. Were you surprised by this statistic? Why or why not?

8. What comes to mind when you hear the word *hell*? Do you think hell is a physical place? What does Santora describe on page 92 as the ultimate purpose of hell? Do you agree or disagree?

9. Do you think it's possible to experience hell before death? Why or why not?

10. Santora quotes C. S. Lewis: "There are only two kinds of people in the end: those who say to God, 'Thy will be done,' and those to whom God says, in the end, '*Thy* will be done.' All that are in Hell, choose it." How did you respond to this quote?

11. What images come to mind when you think of heaven? In chapter 23, Santora describes heaven as a place of responsibility—a place where we are each given things to do. How does this contrast with your view of heaven? What im-

plications does this viewpoint have for our attitudes toward life on earth? What does it say about the ultimate purpose of work?

12. When you imagine meeting God face-to-face after you die, what do you feel? What is the first thing you want to say or do when you see him? How does this desire impact your communication with him now?

13. Santora also describes heaven as the place where God's dreams come true. What are God's dreams for the world? What are God's dreams for your life? Have you ever had a conversation with God about his dreams for you?

14. How do your beliefs about your life source and what happens after death affect the decisions you make today? If God is your life source, are there things you can know with confidence about death? If so, what are they?

15. What is the significance of Jesus' life, death, and resurrection when we consider our own lives and deaths? According to Santora, what makes Christianity different from every other religion, especially as it relates to death (page 222)?

16. Santora says that "what oxygen is to the lungs, hope is to life." What is hope? Why do you think there has been such a fascination with the topic of hope in recent years, both in the media and in political debates? What creates hope?

17. Has reflecting on the topic of death impacted your day-to-day life? If so, what specific changes or decisions have you made? What will you do to sustain those choices?

ALSO BY
FRANK SANTORA:

TURN IT

A DIFFERENT DIRECTION
for a NEW LIFE

FRANK
SANTORA

Available wherever books are sold or at
www.simonandschuster.com

Printed in the United States
By Bookmasters